Penguin Power

DODGER BLUE, HOLLYWOOD LIGHTS, AND MY ONE-IN-A-MILLION BIG LEAGUE JOURNEY

T0356321

Penguin Power

DODGER BLUE, HOLLYWOOD LIGHTS, AND MY ONE-IN-A-MILLION BIG LEAGUE JOURNEY

Ron Cey with Ken Gurnick

TRIUMPH
BOOKS

Library of Congress Cataloging-in-Publication Data

Names: Cey, Ron, author. | Gurnick, Ken, author.
Title: Penguin power: Dodger blue, Hollywood lights, and my
    one-in-a-million big league journey / Ron Cey with Ken Gurnick.
Description: Chicago, Illinois: Triumph Books, [2023]
Identifiers: LCCN 2022052442 | ISBN 9781637273067 (cloth)
Subjects: LCSH: Cey, Ron, | Los Angeles Dodgers (Baseball
    team)—History. | Baseball players—United States—Biography.
Classification: LCC GV865.C49 A3 2023 | DDC 796.357092
    [B]—dc23/eng/20221213
LC record available at https://lccn.loc.gov/2022052442

This book is available in quantity at special discounts for your group or organization. For further information, contact:
Triumph Books LLC
814 North Franklin Street
Chicago, Illinois 60610
(312) 337-0747
www.triumphbooks.com

Printed in U.S.A.
ISBN: 978-1-63727-831-4
Design by Nord Compo

To Fran, my wife of 51 years,
and our children, Daniel and Amanda

CONTENTS

FOREWORD

It is not every day when a baseball player and the team president have a bond of friendship. Out of the hundreds of players who were under my watch as Los Angeles Dodgers president for 28 years, I am happy that Ron Cey and I connected and have been friends for more than 50 years.

He was a thinking man's ballplayer long before analytics swept the game like a wave. That does not mean players in the era of the 1970s and 1980s were any less interested in statistics. Of course they were, but somehow a lot of the instincts of how to play the game seemed to be wired into their DNA, and that eclipsed the numbers. In his own way, Cey was a leader by example—both on and off the field. When he saw something on the team that needed attention, he would take it upon himself to act and find a resolution before it festered.

Cey was destined to become a major league player from a young age. That was his goal. He practiced and worked extremely hard to develop in Little League, high school, college, and through the Dodgers farm system to make it happen. How many of us have a passion that comes to reality? Cey's determination, drive, and work ethic achieved it. As the Dodgers had struggled for many years to find a solution to the revolving door at third base and find stability, Cey's presence was a blessing. To have that position in steady, solid hands was a critical part in the team's decade of success.

Those us of in the front office can learn something from the players. In my case, I was happy to get to know Cey and his wife, Fran, on a personal level. They were very active in giving back to the community in many ways. The Cey family represented the Dodgers with humility, dignity, and class. In 1975 Cey won the first arbitration case against the Dodgers. But there were no hard feelings; it was just part of the business of baseball. That's why it is important for him to share his stories about his experiences as a ballplayer. He offers deep insight into the game, its players, and the extremely important era of the 1970s and early 1980s. That time period is gaining some attention, though significantly less than the so-called golden era, which preceded it.

Dodgers fans will be swept up in the recollections and a telling of history from the man who anchored third base and was a reliable fixture in the heart of the starting lineup. It was always a given that he would be playing and performing to the highest standards. His contributions were significant. From earning walks, scoring runs, hitting home runs, driving in runs, fielding with consistency, Cey was a gamer and as tough as they come. Cey also performed at a high level for the Chicago Cubs. He certainly is one of the all-time great third basemen and has been frequently rated as such. Some of my on-field memories of him include his incredible record-setting month of April of 1977, his exciting grand slam in the 1977 National League Championship Series, and his shocking beaning in Game Five of the 1981 World Series that had everyone concerned for his well-being.

In these pages Cey has given readers a treasure trove into the behind-the-scenes life of a major leaguer from spring training, the grind of the season schedule, travel days, clubhouse life, and meeting celebrities to winning a world championship. The interaction with teammates, the front office, the media, opposing players, and others is all part of this daily life, and Cey chronicles it all. For fans of that Dodgers period—or for those just wanting to learn more about what made the team play in four World Series (1974, 1977, 1978, and 1981) in that time—Cey gives his perspective and honest feelings while contrasting some of the differences in today's game.

I can't think of a better pairing for writing this book than longtime and knowledgeable Dodgers beat writer Ken Gurnick and Dodgers legend Ron Cey. Now it's time to hear from the author, the man himself. Now batting for the Dodgers…No. 10…third baseman…RON CEY.

—Peter O'Malley, Los Angeles Dodgers president, 1970–1998

INTRODUCTION

The doubters said I was stubborn. I'd call it focused. I decided when I was a little kid that I would be a Major League Baseball player. I didn't *want* to be one; I was *going* to be one. It wasn't a dream; it was a mission, and nobody could stop me. From Little League and high school to Washington State University and the minor leagues, every day was a step in my journey. It wasn't easy. It required hard work. And dedication. And the resilience to overcome obstacles.

I wasn't the biggest or strongest or fastest player to come along, but I played 15 seasons in the major leagues. I was a World Series champion, a World Series tri-MVP, and a six-time All-Star. I was one-quarter of the longest-playing infield in history—which debuted more than 50 years ago—and one-quarter of the first 30-homer foursome in history. I set club records and rubbed elbows with famous entertainers. And after my playing days were over, I spent another three decades working on the business side of baseball in sponsorships, promotions, and community relations.

And with all of that behind me, I've written this book to tell the story of Los Angeles' Boys of Summer, another Dodgers team that rose through the minor league system to earn repeated cracks at the World Series before finally winning a championship—just in time before it was broken up. Because it's a story of a personal dream fulfilled, I also hope

13

it inspires others, regardless of their dream, to chase it with passion and everything they've got.

I didn't realize how lucky I was at the time, but when the Dodgers included me in their record-setting amateur draft of 1968, it would form the nucleus of a team that would win over the city of Los Angeles. Before the Lakers and Showtime, before The Great One joined the Kings, and long before the Rams returned to town and won a Super Bowl, the Dodgers from 1974 to 1981 smashed MLB attendance records and appeared in four World Series in eight years.

From the field to the owners' suite, the game today hardly resembles the one we played nearly a half-century ago. But I'm glad I took the bus rides. I hope you enjoy reading what it was like back then as much as I have sharing the memories.

CHAPTER 1

KOUFAX AND THE BOYS OF SUMMER

When the Los Angeles Dodgers beat the Tampa Bay Rays in 2020, it ended a World Series drought for the franchise dating back to 1988. The ceremony afterward was muted because of health protocols, and they never had the downtown parade that we enjoyed in 1981. But the achievement brought great relief to all corners of Dodger Stadium because, frankly, everybody was sick and tired of hearing about the decades-long futility. That was especially true in the clubhouse, as players often expressed dismay that they were being held accountable for earlier failures that had nothing to do with them.

Accountability is in short supply these days. In our time we welcomed it. We won it all in 1981 just in time, as our window of opportunity was closing. We had been knocking on that door in 1974 and 1977 and 1978 and were turned away. Our time was running out, and the only way we could achieve anything close to a "Boys of Summer" status was to knock the door down, walk through it, accomplish it, and close it. And it was very important for us to do that. It solidified all of the great things that went with that period of time. It pretty much solidified the legacy of the infield because second place isn't good enough, you know? The only thing that people remember are the winners, and the yardstick for us was the Brooklyn Dodgers and the Boys of Summer and Sandy Koufax and Don Drysdale, some of the greatest players on the great teams in Dodgers history.

We were driven to reach that level, and as soon as we showed up at Dodgertown, the reminders were everywhere. The streets of the former naval airbase had been renamed after Dodgers Hall of Famers. And if you weren't paying attention to something as obvious as a Hall of Fame name on a street sign, the legacy stared you in the face every single day of spring training on the hallway walls of the buildings at Vero Beach, Florida. Every day we would walk from the dining room to the clubhouse, and the long corridors were lined with murals of game photos of Jackie Robinson, Duke Snider, Roy Campanella, Pee Wee Reese, Gil Hodges, Carl Erskine, Preacher Roe, and I can go on and on and on. You couldn't miss them. It was like a museum in there. When you went to eat, you would pass them. When you went to your room, you would pass them. When you went to the locker room, you would pass them. Intentionally or not, those black-and-white action shots sent a subliminal message. Nobody had to say a word. I remember years later saying to owner Peter O'Malley, "I got the message."

And he said, "What is that?"

I said, "The one that's on the wall every single day as we walk through the halls."

And he started laughing and said, "I'm glad you did. I'm very glad that you did."

It was a constant reminder of what we really anticipated would happen. Not only did I get it, but I also wanted my picture up there as the greatest third baseman in Dodgers history and I wanted pictures of our teams to be up there.

The pictures even came to life. The Dodgers would bring back so many of their great players to be instructors and influencers to the younger players. We grew up with these guys in spring training. They were in our house, or we were in their house, and it was great to have them and their wisdom around. Campanella, who was confined to a wheelchair after a 1958 auto accident, held court with the young catchers in Campy's Bullpen. Dixie Walker worked with the hitters. One week Snider was there or Reese or Erskine.

I remember in the mid-1970s, Koufax would throw batting practice to the position players on the back fields. By that time Koufax had found a role he really seemed to enjoy, being a minor league pitching instructor. It kept him out of the spotlight while helping craft the next generation of Dodgers pitching. The first time I saw him on the mound—fit and looking capable of competing—I thought that was really cool. I was thinking, *I'm gonna take batting practice off him and I'm probably going to take him deep. And I'm probably going to be able to say, "I hit balls out of the ballpark off Sandy Koufax."* I ended up hitting a lot of them, and that was the purpose. It's batting practice, working on repetitions, and Koufax knew that. He was out there to be part of what we were doing to be prepared. There was a certain amount of elation, but more than that, I really admired that he was there for our improvement. He was there to help us. And what was even cooler than the elation was the fact that he didn't have the ego attached to it as others did.

Koufax gladly played the selfless part, helping the hitters practice their swings. He was then in his late 30s, having retired after the 1966 season because of severe elbow arthritis. How was it possible that the great Sandy Koufax would be grooving batting practice fastballs and not be tempted to reach back and blow one by us? Because he didn't have that ego in him. Some pitchers can't dial it back like that. Don Sutton was so competitive that he couldn't or wouldn't throw batting practice during spring training, like the other pitchers. He wanted to beat you on every pitch, even if you were a teammate. He was competitive, and batting practice is completely different than a game. You're just trying to get loose, get your swing right, and see that your timing's there. Koufax's batting practice was exactly what a hitter wanted. We weren't expecting him to crank it up and let one fly.

When author Jane Leavy was writing her book about Koufax, she called and asked me to verify a rumor she heard that when Koufax threw batting practice to us, nobody could hit the ball out of the cage. And I started laughing. He never would have allowed that to happen. And she's like, "You mean it's not true?"

I said, "Of course, it's not true."

Off the field, Koufax and I developed a friendly relationship. He had a home in Vero Beach, and our wives became friends, hanging out during the spring days. That led to us having dinner together a couple times a week. Koufax was always gracious, and we always had a great time together. He's also very generous. A fraternity friend of mine used to shag balls with us during batting practice and he was a big college basketball fan. Koufax played basketball at the University of Cincinnati before he signed with the Dodgers. He got tickets to the Final Four in Seattle and took my buddy with him. Koufax lives on the East Coast, and I don't get a chance to see him much anymore. Koufax has always been like the old E.F. Hutton brokerage commercial. He's always been soft-spoken, but when he speaks, people listen. Young pitchers brave enough to seek advice received it willingly.

Koufax didn't participate in the annual fantasy camps that the Dodgers began holding at Dodgertown in the mid-1980s, but quite a few of the Boys of Summer and early Los Angeles Dodgers did. Drysdale and Erskine, Snider and Reese, Maury Wills and Ralph Branca, among many others, were there. Just like everything else with the Dodgers, fantasy camp assignments were handed off from one generation to another and were one of my most enjoyable assignments. Bill Russell and Reggie Smith were regulars at the fantasy camps in the early 2000s, and when my schedule allowed, I joined them, mixing with the fans and giving them a taste of what spring training was like for a player. One year we had the entire infield participate: me, Garvey, Davey Lopes, and Russell. To a baseball fan and especially one that grew up with our Dodgers generation, going to a fantasy camp and playing against the most enduring and successful infield in major league history had to be an unforgettable experience. I remember Tommy Lasorda pitching in those camp games, and when a camper got a hit off him, Lasorda would start screaming and throw his glove at the guy as he ran to first base. We'd play at Holman Stadium on the same field the big league team played on, sitting in the same dugout. I've often had campers tell me the experience was one of the true highlights of their lives, a reminder of how lucky we are that we play a game that brings so much happiness to so many.

Reese was great at the fantasy camps. Clem Labine was a kick in the pants. Erskine had his stories and played the harmonica. I got him one fantasy camp and I think I might have pissed him off. We were playing his team and we rolled them up pretty good. And at the banquet that night, I got up there and said, "Yeah, the team we were playing today didn't come out with much energy."

And when Erskine got up there, he said, "Don't talk to my team about not having any energy." I started laughing.

I never got close with Snider. He hurt my feelings one time, indirectly, when he told somebody that I wasn't the best third baseman in Dodgers history. I think he said Billy Cox. In my encounters with Snider, he always seemed bothered by the fans. Drysdale was at a few of the early fantasy camps. I never developed a close relationship with him like I did with Koufax, even though Drysdale was still playing when I signed. The only reason I'm sure he knew I existed is that I heard he made a crack about me in the clubhouse. It was my second spring training and I was late again because of my military reserve commitment. Being on the 40-man roster, I had a locker in the major league clubhouse. I was told that one day Drysdale looked over at my locker and said, "You know, this kid's got his name in here on his locker, and I haven't seen him for two years."

Even if you're the punchline to a clubhouse joke, it was a thrill just to be part of an organization that had all this rich history and tradition. We knew that this was available for us if we were good enough. I think a lot of our guys felt that way because we had that mentality. We had won throughout the minor leagues. We were All-Star caliber players on all levels, and I didn't expect anything different. I think I'm one of the only players in the organization's history that won on every single level. And I'm talking about instructional league, winter ball, Single A, Double A, Triple A, everywhere. To me the natural progression was to be an All-Star caliber player on a winning major league team. I wasn't just there to have a job in Major League Baseball. I wanted to be one of those guys. And, fortunately, I was. We had All-Stars all over the diamond. And I think we were ingrained with the belief that we would just keep winning, that it would translate into success on every level. There wasn't anything to really deter us. And, of course, we were under the wing of Lasorda, and that was also a good thing because he kept instilling in us that we were the cream of the crop.

The tradition of winning Dodgers baseball dated to Branch Rickey and the late 1940s. We were the Dodgers and we had an expectation of winning. We didn't rebuild. We weren't a team in the cellar, hoping to go .500 the next year. When we went to spring training, the only thing we thought of from Day One was bringing home the big trophy. I've had conversations with players on other clubs that didn't have this singular concept of winning. They were hoping to hang in there the best they could. They didn't have enough talent. Maybe subconsciously they didn't believe they could beat us. Sometimes if you believe you are the better team, you can get complacent. But we turned that around. We felt that other teams had extra motivation to beat us, and that helped keep us on our toes all the time. We couldn't just throw our gloves out there and have the ball roll in. We had to play hard. We didn't want to let anybody think they had an opportunity to beat us. That's just the way we lived. It was all documented in Al Campanis' book, *The Dodger Way to Play Baseball.*

That's part of the legend that goes with it. When we took the field in batting practice, we had a following. And we wanted to show people how we did things when we took the field. I remember the other dugouts weren't empty when we took batting practice. Instead of going back into the clubhouse, they were watching to see how we did things and learned from it. We had an influence and an impact. When we finally beat the New York Yankees in the 1981 World Series, the narrative was that it was revenge for losing to the Yankees in 1977 and 1978. Yeah, it was extra sweet. It sounds a lot better when you say you beat the Yankees because of their history and tradition.

• CHAPTER 2 •

THE EARLY YEARS

I was first drafted out of high school in the 24th round by the New York Mets in 1966, but that wasn't the only draft I was paying attention to. The Vietnam War was raging in the mid-1960s. Thousands of young Americans were dying halfway around the world for reasons that teenagers like me (and a lot of grown-ups) just couldn't understand. It wasn't like 9/11, when our country was attacked and we went to war. Guerilla warfare in the Vietnam jungles seemed senseless to most of us. I didn't find it very appealing to become another casualty. The law stated that American men between the ages of 18–26 must serve 21 months in the military. Available to us at the time was an educational deferment that delayed service for four years while you attended college full time. With the college scholarship I was offered by Washington State, I was eligible for a student deferment. I was fortunate to have that option and I chose to accept the deferment and go to school instead of signing with the Mets. I planned to then enlist in the reserves to satisfy my service requirement, minimizing the chances that I would be sent to Vietnam. Had I decided to sign and play professionally instead of taking the student deferment, I would have been classified 1A and then would have gone to Advanced Individual Training and, likely, been on my way to Vietnam.

It was an easy choice. I would be eligible for the baseball draft after two college years at age 20. It happened to some of the kids I went to school with. When you turned 18, you had to register with the Selective Service System, which conducted a birthdate lottery. And if your birth-date came up among the early numbers, you were off to war. That's exactly what happened to Roy Gleason in 1967. He was in Los Angeles Dodgers spring training; got his draft notice; was sent from Vero Beach, Florida, to the front lines in March; and in July of 1968 suffered shrapnel wounds to his arm and leg, effectively ruining his baseball career. The military draft was a roll of the dice and a life gamble I wanted no part of. My dream was to play professional baseball. So I went to Washington State, knowing I would get an education while still serving my country through six years of reserve duty.

Going to college was my first real time away from home. My world had been pretty sheltered. My first airplane flight wasn't until I was 18 years old. College allowed me the needed time to adjust to being on my own, to get an education I could fall back on if baseball didn't work out (not that I ever considered that possibilty) while playing baseball in arguably the best conference at the time, then called the Pacific-8. Hopefully, I would be in a better position for the baseball draft after collegiate competition than I was coming out of high school. My coach at Washington State, Chuck Brayton, was a local legend. He coached there for 33 seasons and had the fourth-highest win total of any college coach at the time he retired. His teams finished first 11 years in a row, the first while I played for him, which I considered a fortunate honor.

Little-known fact, but Coach Brayton is the one who nicknamed me "Penguin." It wasn't Tommy Lasorda, no matter how often he tried to take credit for it. I had the nickname before Lasorda ever knew I existed. It was Coach Brayton who said when I ran the bases my motion was more like a Penguin waddle than a stride, and the tag not only stuck, but it also became an asset, even leading to the theme of a Nike poster.

I enjoyed needling Lasorda, arguing how he wasn't the first. He always insisted he was.

Coach Brayton was always looking out for his players and he tried to talk me out of signing when the Dodgers drafted me in the third round of my sophomore season. Obviously, he wanted to keep together a team that had just finished first. But I think he also honestly believed I might need one more year just to refine my skills and improve my draft value. As much as I admired Coach and respected his opinion, I was itching to be a pro. I was further encouraged when the USC baseball coach, the legendary Rod Dedeaux, told Brayton he thought I was the best unsigned hitter in America. It's probably the strongest compliment I ever received. Dick Calvert was the Dodgers' Washington area scout, and Bill Brenzel was his scouting supervisor. They were the ones who convinced Dodgers management to include me in the 1968 draft. Calvert later became a broadcasting legend for the University of Nevada, Las Vegas. Scouts like Calvert and Benzel have a thankless job, and players often forget that their careers might never have happened without the tireless work these scouts put in. I am eternally grateful that they stuck their necks out for me.

After I signed, Calvert even drove me for three-and-a-half hours across Washington state from Tacoma to Tri-Cities, the Dodgers' rookie league affiliate where I was assigned, for my first day on the job. My manager there was Don "Ducky" LeJohn, who you've probably never heard of. That's unfortunate because the Don LeJohns are the backbone of our sport. He only had a cup of coffee in the major leagues, making an appearance in the 1965 World Series. But his real contribution was toiling for 20 seasons as a manager in the Dodgers' minor league system. He managed nearly 2,500 games from 1967 to 1986. Pretty much every player that came through the system during that span was shaped in some way by Ducky LeJohn, and I was no exception. From Day One, I think Ducky was in my corner. He told me he liked what he saw in my play early on. Goldie Holt, who was one of our cross-checking scouts back then, filed a solid report after watching me play and was always in my corner.

I felt like I was in a good spot. The Tri-Cities Atoms, supposedly nicknamed for the top-secret plutonium production facility nearby, were a good club. We had two other players from the '68 draft that had significant big league careers as far as time and performance: Joe Ferguson and Doyle Alexander. Ferguson led the Northwest League in home runs that year, anchoring the middle of the lineup, and for several years was an offensive force for the Dodgers. Alexander didn't pitch long for the Dodgers, but he spent 19 years in the major leagues. The rest of the higher draft picks were sent to the rookie league affiliate at Ogden, a team that had finished first in back-to-back seasons under the direction of a squatty former pitcher and scout named Tommy Lasorda. We were good at Tri-Cities, but the Ogden group always got top billing and the bigger-named prospects, including Bobby Valentine, Bill Buckner, Steve Garvey, Tom Paciorek, Sandy Vance, Bob Gallagher, and Bruce Ellingsen. I can't explain how they decided which of us would play where. I know that they wanted to split Garvey and me because we both signed as third basemen. He went to one place, and I went to the other. Altogether, we comprised the greatest draft in history. And if Valentine hadn't had that ugly accident playing for the Angels, snapping his leg running into the outfield fence in Anaheim, he would have been a key major leaguer as well.

Going into my draft season, I was confident there would be increased interest because I had a big freshman season and two summers playing for the semi-pro Cheney Studs in the Seattle area. The Studs were an elite team that recruited actively and were the two-time West Coast champions, earning a berth in the Stan Musial World Series in Battle Creek, Michigan.

In 1966 I had a monster World Series. I went 6-for-6 in the first game of that World Series and ended the tournament hitting .625 (15-for-24), and we lost to a Dallas team in the final game. The next year in the World Series, I hit .385 (5-for-13). I caught a glimpse from a number of MLB franchises, and that tournament was the first time I ran into longtime Dodgers minor league advisor Guy Wellman, another front-office member I had a chance to impress. After that first World Series, I reported to WSU for a full week of fall practice to play freshman baseball, hitting .396 on the season. In the summer with the Studs, we won the regional and West Coast playoffs and went back to Battle Creek for another World Series. Returning from the previous year's near-miss, we drew our share of attention. Our best pitcher, Rick Austin, parlayed the exposure into being a first-round pick of the Detroit Tigers. I was the most closely-followed position player. I was confident I had improved my draft status despite the fact that while playing in the Northwest we were limited to only 38 games. Weather in Washington was always an issue. I remember playing games in the snow. We had trouble getting our games in and we didn't have a schedule where we would, say, go to Arizona for 10 days and play everybody every day to get games under our belt. We didn't have the same benefit of sunbelt teams in Arizona and Florida that were playing close to 80 games. I mean, 80 games? We figured there was no way they were even going to school; they were just playing ball every day.

Our time to shine was during a California swing, a week when we'd play Stanford and Cal in the north and USC and UCLA in the south. In 1968 that California swing made my season and probably moved me up on the draft boards because I tore it up. Against Cal I went 4-for-9 with a couple doubles. The next day we went to Stanford to face Vance, who would eventually be one of my major league teammates. At the time he was the No. 1 pitcher for Stanford, the top-ranked baseball team in the nation. Don Rose, who went on to pitch for the Angels, was also in their rotation. Bob Boone was playing third base. Gallagher was playing center field. Mark Marquess was playing first base. He became the Stanford coach for more than 40 years during a legendary career. I got two hits in this game, including the winning home run in the ninth inning. From there we traveled to UCLA for a doubleheader, and I went 5-for-8 with a double and home run. The next day across town at USC, we lost in 13 innings on a pop fly over that short porch in right field at Bovard Field.

Overall, that swing established Washington State as a legitimate team, and I made a name as a player. I don't think I had anything fewer than two hits in each game. I was driving in runs and hitting the ball hard and hitting a few home runs and I know the Dodgers were there. I know Dodgers general manager Al Campanis came to watch us play the UCLA game, and he was very impressed from what I had heard. Coming off that California swing, I had confidence going into the draft. I was getting a lot of publicity. I was having a big year. I was our No. 1 hitter. I tied for the conference lead in home runs and was second in RBIs. So even though Coach Brayton told me I might need another year, I was pretty sure I was going to be drafted high and I was ready to sign this time.

The Dodgers drafted me in the third round of the secondary phase in 1968. Calvert and Benzel came to our house and signed me for a $21,000 bonus. The structure of the MLB draft has changed remarkably since then. But to put that signing bonus in today's perspective, I was the 53rd overall selection in my draft. The 53rd overall selection in the 2022 draft signed for $1.25 million. Guess I was born too early.

The Dodgers had a vast scouting network and selected players from all over the country. When I got to Tri-Cities, I hadn't previously known any of my teammates. Although I would later play in the big leagues with Tri-Cities teammates Ferguson and Alexander, one player from our draft I might have known the best was Bill Buckner, even though I didn't meet him until the next year. That's because his brother, Bobby Buckner, was a teammate in Tri-Cities. Bobby Buckner was a pretty good player at that level. But he was always telling me about his younger brother, Bill, who was the real star of the family. Billy was playing for Lasorda in Ogden and was on fire. When our season at Tri-Cities was done in early September, I had to be back in school and maintain my GPA to retain my reserve military status. After I was done with reserve training in March, I went to L.A. for the flight to Florida. By that time spring training had already begun. So because of the military training, I was late. I wasn't alone. Bill Buckner was finished with his classes at USC and he was Florida-bound as well. We were both called to L.A. and given instructions to report to the Dodgers-owned plane at LAX.

This was the plane used to fly the Dodgers around the country for road trips during the season. It was an old Boeing 720, customized to serve the entire traveling party of players, coaches, staff, and media. It was customized with card tables, first-class seats throughout, better food than minor leaguers ever taste, and a help-yourself buffet of snacks. It wasn't a small plane. But for this trip, in addition to the pilot, copilot, and flight attendant, there were only three passengers—me, Bill Buckner, and our chaperone, Marge Roundtree, the executive secretary for General Manager Campanis. That's when I met Bill Buckner. We talked the entire flight and really bonded. Even though we were teammates for only four years in Los Angeles and were reunited for two seasons with the Chicago Cubs, he was my closest friend in the game. His reputation was tarnished by one haunting play in the 1986 World Series, but he deserved better than that. He was a great hitter, a loyal friend, and since his tragic death in 2019 from Lewy body dementia, I miss him terribly.

That first spring at Dodgertown, I hung out with Buckner, Valentine, and Paciorek, and those were some of the greatest times of my life. Dodgertown was unlike any other team's spring training complex. During World War II, it was a naval air base—complete with barracks that had neither heat nor air conditioning. Because the Dodgers had more minor league affiliates (26) than any other major league franchise, they needed a complex large enough to serve them. The site had been given back to the city of Vero Beach by the government after the war ended and had become an abandoned white elephant. With an airport literally within walking distance of the practice fields, housing for upwards of 600 players, and a mess hall to feed them, Dodgers visionary executive Branch Rickey saw its potential. I use the word "housing" loosely because we lived in those barracks with mosquito screens, overhead fans, and a community shower. There was one telephone located at the main entrance, and every call had to go through a switchboard. You'd wait in line until it was your turn to make the call. It sounds crazy now when even elementary school kids have cellphones, but that's how it was. We ate in the old mess hall about a block away from the barracks. Vero Beach has become an appealing location for second homes on Florida's Treasure Coast, but it was a little backwater town back then with one traffic light. The largest employer was the Piper Aircraft Company. When we wanted to go somewhere, we usually rode bikes. Nothing was very far away because there really wasn't anything there. After workouts we liked to go for a bike ride, stop at the Dairy Queen, and just ride along and survey the territory and horse around without getting into too much trouble. Needless to say, it was a simpler time.

The Dodgers took over the naval base in 1948. The previous spring they trained in Havana, Cuba, making it easier to keep secret Rickey's plan to integrate the game with the arrival of Jackie Robinson. Part-owner

Walter O'Malley bought out Rickey in 1950 and began a perpetual upgrade project to ensure the Dodgers had the finest self-contained spring facility in the game. Vero Beach was so thrilled to have such a high-profile tenant for the abandoned air base that the rent was $1 a year. Along with the glory and fame of a Major League Baseball team, O'Malley brought with him the family atmosphere that made being a Dodger truly unique.

O'Malley went to great lengths to make Dodgertown enjoyable, but he couldn't do much about the humidity. I remember my very first day at full spring training in 1969. I went from my home state of Washington, where it's cool, to Florida, where it's hot and humid. I had never been in weather like that. We broke for lunch at noon, and I was coming off Field 1 and just puked everything out. Roundtree, Campanis' secretary, walked out of the clubhouse right then and said, "Oh, my God, are you okay?"

It was pathetic. And for conditioning they made you run laps around the place, and I was never a jogger. My normal workouts were for quick reactions, sprinting, or running short distances at top speed. This jogging was not up my alley. Veteran pitcher Claude Osteen ran by me and said something like, "It looks like you're having a tough day there."

I actually kind of resented that because it wasn't meant sympathetically. It sounded more pointed like, "You're not gonna make it."

I missed all of spring training in 1970 doing my military reserve training. I began basic training in December in Texas and didn't show up in Florida until May. I was expecting to advance that season to (Double A) Albuquerque, but because I was trying to play catch-up, Albuquerque manager Del Crandall came to me and said, "I think it'd be a good idea if you went down to [Single A] Bakersfield and started playing every day."

I was disappointed because I thought Crandall was a little bit condescending to me under the circumstances. I didn't appreciate the fact that he was trying to frame me as a player based on two weeks of extended spring training in 1970. But it was probably the right decision. I went down to Bakersfield and I hit .331 with 22 home runs in 98 games there. All my stats across the board were good, and I jumped to the 40-man roster for the 1971 season.

The previous year, I was a late-season call-up. Trust me: it was the same scenario as the year before. I had no spring training and I finally got to Albuquerque after its season started and almost immediately hurt my hip in the batter's box swinging. I just ripped something and fell straight down. It felt like I tore the ball-and-socket joint in my hip. This injury stayed with me for most of the year probably because we did almost nothing medically for it. Day after day after day, it was: go to the clubhouse, see the trainer, get in the whirlpool. We didn't have a specialist look at it. We didn't do anything, and that prolonged it. I was getting frustrated by it, and even worse, the manager was getting frustrated by it. I was getting closer to being able to play and then had a setback, and Crandall came to me kind of disgusted and he said, "When do you think you're going to play?" It wasn't like, "Geez I'm really sorry about the setback." It was more like, "When is this going to be done?"

I felt bad about it, but there wasn't really much I could do about it. I started to come around after that and was able to hit for average but didn't have any power. My lower body was still healing. I didn't have the drive from my legs. In the playoffs I hit a couple of home runs so I knew that I was starting to come along, and we won the Texas League championships, but it didn't keep them from taking me off the major league roster. That wasn't all bad because it meant when I got to spring training in 1971, I'd be working with Lasorda, who was promoted to manage Triple A that season. I had played well for him in instructional league, and he already had a chance to see me up close and personal and was in my corner. I felt with Lasorda that I was in a good place. When Lasorda saw me at spring training in 1971, he said something that might have changed my career trajectory. He said, "Look, don't worry about a thing here. You're going to be my third baseman, and I don't give a shit if you get a base hit all spring."

There really is nothing better for a player to hear. This was going to be my first full spring training, and I had a chance to showcase myself and make a big impression without the pressure of winning a job. I could just play my game. The previous year was a fluke, I believed that completely. I just had to re-establish who I was as a player. And with the confidence Lasorda showed in me, I had a great spring training and was ready to go out of the blocks when our season opened at Triple A Spokane. I rewarded Tommy's confidence that year, hitting .328 with 32 home runs and leading the league with 123 RBIs in 130 games. And I must admit I was so focused on re-establishing myself that I sort of forgot about the bigger picture.

Because one night in Spokane, Washington, in late August, Lasorda said he wanted to go to lunch the next day with me and Elton Schiller, our general manager. The season was to end in just a few days, and Lasorda wanted to have lunch with me? I didn't get it. Usually, we went to lunch while the club was on the road, not at home. So I asked, "What's the big deal about lunch?"

Annoyed, he said, "Will you just come to lunch?"

Arguing with Lasorda was usually a waste of time, so I went to lunch, and we were sitting there, and it wasn't long before he said, "Hey, I just want to let you know that in a couple days you're going to be on a plane going to Los Angeles."

And I was just a blockhead. I was kind of naïve and I didn't realize what he was saying. I actually had no idea what he was talking about. My mind-set the whole year was trying to re-establish myself in their minds. I wasn't waiting for a call-up. I thought he was joking. And part of that, which he didn't know or realize, was that I was getting married that weekend, as soon as the Spokane season ended. So I asked him how I was going to be on a plane to Los Angeles on September 2 and on another plane to Chicago on September 8 for my wedding and then rejoin the team in San Francisco? Within a few days, I had the two most important days of my life in front of me. He said not to worry about it. "I'll tell Al [Campanis], and we'll find a way," Lasorda said. "You'll get to Chicago, you'll get married, and everything will be fine."

It was stressful but in a good way. I flew to L.A., and the Dodgers put me up in a little hotel off the Sunset Strip. I was sitting in the lobby, wearing a suit, and got antsy. I had never been to Dodger Stadium and didn't want to sit in the hotel lobby anymore. So I got a cab and headed for the ballpark. If you've never been to Dodger Stadium, they built it into the side of a mountain in a ravine. Driving through the main gate, you see the hills and palm trees, and suddenly the stadium unfolds before you. I thought, *Geez, look at this place.* I got the chills. They let me off at the top of the park, which is eight levels up right behind home plate, looking out at the field and the mountain backdrop. It was awesome. I took the elevator down to the clubhouse level and I walked in and I saw Buck and Valentine and Wimpy (Paciorek's nickname). I didn't realize that we all got called up together.

The club was in a pennant race at that time—four or five or six games out—and we didn't get much of a chance to play. I got two pinch-hitting appearances. Mostly, we just twiddled our thumbs. But at least we were there. I vividly remember Dick Allen on that club, and he was a character. I had a lot of fun talking with him. He was a guy who didn't take batting practice, but there wasn't a defiance to go with it. He wasn't making enemies. But Walt Alston had rules, and they wanted you to play by their rules. So there was always a little tension. Allen was an established player, a terrific player. He swung a 36 or 38 ounce bat and he had all the whip action that you could imagine and he used to just bury balls straight away. I remember a night when he hit three balls to the center-field fence, and each one got run down and caught. You do that once and you come back upset and throw a helmet or kick something. He did it three times and he came back and sat right down next to me and said, "You know, I can't believe I miscalculated three in one night."

I wouldn't have come back with a sense of humor like that, but that's what made him rock and roll. He wasn't as big as I thought, but he was cut. He was a masher and he was unforgettable. That was my indoctrination to Allen, one of my all-time favorite teammates.

What did my 1971 season at Triple A Spokane—including a September call-up to Los Angeles and instructional league in Arizona—get me for 1972? It got me a trip back to Triple A, where I spent another whole season and hit .329 with 23 home runs and 103 RBIs and 117 walks. Lasorda later told me he had been asking Campanis to promote me that whole season. Lasorda knew that I felt I had spent more time in the minor leagues than I needed to. What else did I have to do? I was overqualified. There shouldn't have been any issue about this, but Campanis was still a little reluctant. I wasn't the first player in the Dodgers system who felt he had spent too much time in the minor leagues. In 1982, for example, Mike Marshall was coming off winning the Triple Crown in the PCL as the Minor League Player of the Year and was ready to play first base in the major leagues, but Steve Garvey was blocking him, and Marshall went back to Triple A, as if he had anything left to prove there. Greg Brock, who was one year behind Marshall, also played first base and he slugged 44 homers at Triple A in 1982. So the Dodgers had two guys ready at first base, but they had a perennial All-Star ahead of them in Garvey, who finally left as a free agent after the 1982 season. That's when Brock took over first base, and Marshall was moved to the outfield.

Anyway, Campanis wasn't really quite sold on whether I was the answer in 1972. And I felt like I spent a year longer in the minor leagues because of it. Campanis actually screwed me over. I had a confrontation with him and I left the 1972 spring training and went home. And I told Lasorda that Campanis basically told me the job was mine to lose and that I had a solid first exhibition game—doubled off the wall, drove in a run, scored a run—and felt good about it. Then I didn't start another game. This lasted for about two weeks, and I asked for a meeting.

And Campanis wouldn't take the meeting. Back then I was taking my salary over the course of the year, maybe $12,000 spread over the 12 months. While we're in spring training, I got a pay stub from the office in L.A. with a paycheck deduction I did not understand. So I called Irene Tanji in the payroll office in L.A. and asked her about the deduction and she said, "Oh, that's a state of New Mexico deduction."

And I'm saying to myself, *We're in Florida, and now I realize, New Mexico. They've already sent me out.* And I was in disbelief at this point. I cornered Campanis, and he finally took this meeting. We were five minutes into it, and he got a call and he said, "I have to take this, okay?" He took the call, then came back into the room, and he said, "I'm going to dinner now and we're finished."

And he was with his wife. So I said, "That's it?"

And he said, "Yes, that's it."

So, I decided to go home. He screwed me big time. He was lying to me the entire time. I told Lasorda, "They've already sent me out. I confirmed it. They're already taking New Mexico taxes out of my paychecks."

Lasorda said, "Okay, let me go talk to Al." Campanis was Lasorda's mentor, so they were close. I don't know what he said to Campanis, but Lasorda came back and said, "You go home. But I want you in Albuquerque by this date. And I want you to have this shit worked out. I don't want you coming to Albuquerque feeling sour. So go home and cool off."

I left Vero Beach and went back to Scottsdale, where my wife, Fran, was going to grad school at Arizona State. I would go over to the baseball field at ASU, and the Sun Devils baseball coach, Hall of Famer Bobby Winkles, would open it up for us. I spent the better part of two weeks over there while everybody else was training in Florida. A couple of times, I just went to a public batting cage. Essentially, it was another character test. I'm going to have to do it again and show you I'm the real deal. And I did what Lasorda asked: I showed up in Albuquerque and I had another big year, and we went to the Pacific Coast League championships that year. I learned discipline at the plate that year. I was more patient and set a record for walks. That part of it was good. And then we went to the Triple A World Series in Hawaii. And then about 10 of us got called up, and we had about two weeks of big league games to make a statement.

After my cup of coffee with the Dodgers at the end of the 1972 season, I headed to the Puerto Rican Winter League, playing for a team in Santurce under manager Frank Robinson. The other young Dodgers went to Santo Domingo in the Dominican Republic and played for Lasorda, and we ended up playing each other in the Caribbean World Series in Caracas, Venezuela. We had Willie Crawford. We had Alexander. We had Mike Strahler. Don Baylor was on the team. Tony Perez was on the team—along with Juan Pizzaro and Roger Moret. Juan Beniquez was our shortstop, and Elrod Hendricks was our catcher. Major leaguers Bob Reynolds, Ron Woods, Jerry DaVanon were also there. It was an important next step in my journey.

I don't think I realized it at the time, but the Dodgers' minor league system was designed to weed out players with anything less than top talent. I was naïve and just considered my time in the minors as paying dues until I became a major leaguer. I probably didn't appreciate how talented our organization was. I didn't recognize that there were a lot of players who were just as sure as I was of having success, but they wouldn't make it. I played on teams that won at every level. I was an All-Star at every level.

There wasn't anything deterring my thoughts of working my way up the ladder and playing Major League Baseball. I didn't really have any other goals but to be a major leaguer, and it was only a matter of time. I knew after being drafted that I had to work a lot more, probably more on the defensive side of things because I felt that I was going to hit. I needed the repetitions in the field. As young kids we just cared about hitting. It wasn't like we would dedicate one day to defense and not pick up the bats. As I got further along—not only through college but into the minor leagues—I was improving defensively but not to a point where I felt like I was as polished a player with the glove as I was with the bat. You could have said that about a lot of players who focused on hitting. They don't pay for your glove. I knew I needed to work on defense and I wanted that experience before I got to the major leagues because I certainly didn't want to go up there and be overwhelmed defensively. I felt that I had good throwing accuracy and good hands. I didn't have a great arm. My foot speed was average by major league standards. Because I ran like a penguin or was associated with that, I think there was a little bit of an assumption that I couldn't run from here to there. It was the only negative to my nickname. The nickname was catchy, I'll say that.

After my second year at Triple A, I figured there really wasn't anything left for me to do in the minor leagues. It was my time, and in 1973 I made the club out of spring training. Ken McMullen started the first six games at third base that year, but he hurt his back, and that lingered all season, limiting him to only 46 games. McMullen's injury was my opportunity, and eventually I took over for him, while Davey Lopes took over at second base for Lee Lacy. That rookie season I had a good first half, and we were right there in the standings. I was on pace to hit .300 with 20 home runs and 100 RBIs. Being Rookie of the Year was becoming realistic until the whole thing kind of fell apart. I hit .266 with a .782 OPS in the first half but .203 and .617 in the second half. I was really disappointed. I ended up being the Dodgers Rookie of the Year, the top rookie third baseman on the Topps list, and set a club record with 80 RBIs for a rookie, but I really was not happy. It was my awakening that this was a different level, and you have to keep your head down and keep pushing from the first day to the last day of the season. I had things to work on and really needed to make this effort to get back on track.

I went to spring training the next year, and we were over in Tampa for an exhibition game against the Cincinnati Reds. It's almost like Perez—because of our relationship as teammates in Puerto Rico—read my mind. I got to first base, and with no prompting, he said, "Got to play a full year. Got to play a full year. Right?"

And I smiled and said, "You hit my nerve."

• CHAPTER 3 •

Alston, Lasorda, Campanis, and The Dodger Way

If there was one essential element in the Dodgers' success under the O'Malley ownership it was stability, and nothing epitomized stability better than the tenured leadership of Hall of Fame field managers Walt Alston and Tommy Lasorda and general manager Al Campanis.

Hired in 1954 by Brooklyn general manager Buzzie Bavasi, Alston served 23 seasons as the Dodgers' skipper. Lasorda, hired by Campanis to replace Alston at the end of the 1976 season, managed in Los Angeles for 21 years. Campanis, whose otherwise distinguished career was destroyed by one late-night television interview, spent nearly 50 years in the Dodgers organization as a player, manager, coach, scout, scouting director and then nearly two decades as Bavasi's successor as general manager.

Each had brief and unsuccessful careers as major league players. Alston had one big league at-bat: a strikeout. Lasorda pitched in 26 major league games and was 0–4 with a 6.48 ERA. Campanis played in seven games for Brooklyn during World War II and had a .100 batting average.

Yet, from the mid-1950s until the mid-1990s, every player that wore the Dodgers uniform owed a debt to at least one of them or, in my case, all three. I was drafted by Campanis and played for Alston and Lasorda. Campanis knew talent and how to acquire it; Alston and Lasorda knew what to do with it. Campanis combined Branch Rickey's old-school fundamentals with visionary adaptability. When most clubs ignored the Caribbean, he found and signed Roberto Clemente, who the Dodgers later lost to the Pittsburgh Pirates in the Rule 5 draft, then had protégé Ralph Avila build a state-of-the-art baseball training academy in the Dominican Republic that became the model of the industry. When MLB tried to discourage the signing of "bonus babies" by requiring them to go directly to the major leagues, Campanis discovered and signed Sandy Koufax. Then to make room for Koufax on the roster, he sent down another left-hander, Lasorda. Faced with rebuilding the Dodgers after Koufax retired, Campanis learned from NFL peers how to prepare for baseball's new amateur draft. I respected the no-nonsense Alston, I appreciated the baseball acumen of Campanis, and I was eternally grateful to Lasorda.

Alston and I actually had a really good relationship. My first recollection was my first year on the 25-man roster, and I was finally getting an opportunity. I had just come back from Puerto Rico, where I played for Frank Robinson, and I had a little mustache. The Dodgers had a rule: no facial hair, and Alston came to me at some point in spring training and said, "I'd really like you to shave your mustache." And being kind of the new kid on the block, I didn't have any issues with it. I just went ahead and did it. I went out and performed my rookie year, but two things came up.

There was a play in a game, where I made a mental mistake with runners on base, and it put us in jeopardy, and I knew it as soon as it happened. A ball was chopped at me with runners on first and second, and I thought I was going to be able to make a tag play on the runner coming down from second base, and he eluded me. So, I did a full circle and threw to first base, and it was too late, and everybody was safe.

When you're a rookie, you don't always have everything plugged into your brain. I hesitated just enough to where all runners were going to be safe. And I believe we got out of it, but it was the idea that physical mistakes happen, but mental mistakes have to be kept at a real minimum, or you put your team in jeopardy. Afterward I wasn't feeling so great about this play, and, sure enough, Alston was passing through the clubhouse and he stopped by my locker. And he said to me, "Do you suppose you can come in a little bit early tomorrow? I want to talk to you about something."

And so I said, "Sure, of course, what time you want me to be here?"

We set a time. I went home and didn't sleep too well because I was wondering what was going to happen. *Is he going to just come in and tear me apart for making that play? Is he going to sit me down?* I got to the park early because I was a little antsy about this meeting. Eventually, the time came, and I went in and, in a very short period of time, I realized that he wasn't going to be calling me out. We were going to actually have a conversation about this. So that took some of my anxiety away. And then he got into the play, and I owned it, that it was my fault. He asked me to explain what I was thinking at the time, and we talked it out. He said, "Okay, you've probably thought that you might not be playing tonight, but you're going to make some mistakes and you're not going to sit down every time you make a mistake. You're going to play and you're going to continue to play and just keep learning and keep working hard."

I was relieved. It was a great conversation to have. I had a great deal more respect for him after that because of the way he handled that situation. I was a young player, and he could have ripped me apart, could have hurt me, but he didn't. Instead, he pumped me up. I really felt he was in my corner, and he entrusted a lot in me, and I'm grateful for that. He won me over with that one, and it helped my maturation process tremendously.

There was a second time that Alston brought me in for a meeting, and it wasn't for a screw-up. He said, "You're probably the most selective hitter on the team. And that's certainly an asset, but here's one thing I would like for you to think about: when we have men on base and it's less than two outs—and only if you're comfortable with it—I want you to expand your strike zone because I want you to drive that run in. I don't want it to go past you. And if you mess it up, it's on me."

I felt like, *Wow, he's giving me a green light here.* And of course, I had to be selective about those pitches that I would expand my zone on and where they were. So I had to kind of experiment a little bit with that, too. But I told that story to Joey Amalfitano, who was our third-base coach under Lasorda, and he just about fell off his chair. He said, "Wow, what a vote of confidence." I was only in my second full season at the time, but Alston had a growing trust in me.

The difference between Alston and Lasorda was night and day, black and white. Alston was a very calm and collected manager who kept things pretty much close to the vest. If he had something to say to you, he'd take you aside and have a private conversation, man to man. Lasorda was loud and had to be the center of attention, cracking jokes, telling stories, hugging everybody he saw. They couldn't have had more different personality types. One thing they had in common was that they weren't star players in their day, and I think that made them better managers. They knew how hard the game was to play at the highest level because they couldn't. They understood that failure was a major part of our game. I think that made them a little more patient and a little less demanding.

Another memory of Alston was a doubleheader against the Reds in Cincinnati in '75. I went 5-for-5 in the first game with three doubles and hit everything on the screws. In the second game, I lined out to Pete Rose at third, lined out to Doug Flynn at short. Ken Griffey Sr. ran down a sinking liner in right-center field and picked it off the shoe tops. Approaching the top of the ninth inning, I was walking toward the bat rack preparing to hit, and Alston was looking at me as I was walking down the dugout. He had a smile on his face, and I didn't know why he was smiling at me. I was 0-for-3 with three rockets, so I wasn't real happy regardless of what happened in the first game. He put his hand on my shoulder and said, "Hey, would you do me a favor? Just hit one more line drive."

For Alston, that was dugout humor. And it kind of loosened me up a little bit. And what did I do? I went up and hit one more line drive, but this one actually got through. I finished the day 6-for-9, and Vin Scully said they were nine of the hardest hit balls he'd ever seen hit by one person in a doubleheader. When I got to first base after the last one, Tony Perez said, "Are you okay, man? Are you sure you're all right? You're not running a temperature or anything?" He got me laughing.

We acted more conservatively under Alston. With Lasorda, we hugged each other more and celebrated a little bit more, which was probably a little bit out of step with old-school baseball. Our team, and primarily Glenn Burke and Dusty Baker, is credited with inventing the high-five. But nobody wanted to get their feelings hurt and nobody wanted to embarrass or upstage anybody back then. Because if a guy hit a home run and Bob Gibson was on the mound, I wouldn't suggest that he celebrate too much running around. I would suggest not doing a bat flip at home plate and then make it around the bases in slow motion and then cross yourself when you get to home plate and raise your hands to the sky and tip your hat and point to people in the luxury suite. Because the next time you would be facing Gibson, you'd end up in the dirt, if not the hospital. We celebrated when and how it was appropriate.

Mostly, we'd do it in the clubhouse. We didn't need to do it in the opponent's face. Sports now are so different. A defensive lineman gets a sack and jumps up and down and flexes and what not. A shooter makes a three-pointer and he's clowning down to the other side of the court. In baseball, bats are flipped, and pitchers are fist-pumping strike-outs. Fernando Rodney would give that bow-and-arrow pose after a save. These guys are having fun. As a player in my day, it wouldn't have been tolerated. Now, as a fan, I don't mind it so much because it makes the game more entertaining to watch. In a way I kind of wish we had celebrated to loosen things up a little bit more during our time.

Lasorda was exactly the right guy at the right time for our young group. He was the one who molded us, and that's why he deserves a lot of credit. I still believe that was his greatest skill: identifying the best potential and instilling in us the confidence to bring it out. And within the organization, he stood up for us and he fought for us. You needed a guy back then to help bang the drum for you with the executives. It was like having a public-relations person in the front office. The work that you're doing sometimes isn't enough. We needed him to hype us a little bit and stick his neck out for us and we all benefitted. He was a minor league manager with whatever destiny he had in front of him, and our success helped catapult him into a legend, a World Series winner, a Hall of Famer, and an Olympic gold medalist.

Some criticize Lasorda for being a promoter, but those critics ignore his tireless work ethic. That was never stressed in the narrative of his story, but it was as much the reason for his success as anything. He worked around the clock. He was with us all the time. He threw batting practice for hours and would proudly demand to have the lights turned on at Holman Stadium in Vero Beach to continue the workout. He was never off duty—whether we were at the ballpark or away from it. We'd go to the racetrack or a movie to kill a few hours. And everybody knows about Lasorda's appetite. We ate together—often for free—and in Italian fashion, it wasn't just a meal but a bonding event. That was the way he nurtured his team. Every Sunday in spring training, we played a day game at Holman Stadium and after the game would go over to the bowling alley with our group of Lasorda guys. And we'd go to the smorgasbord at the Holiday Inn across from the Ocean Grill in Vero Beach and afterward to the Dairy Queen on the way back to Dodgertown.

It was good, clean fun, but it also was a master's degree in connecting. It was just another example of what Lasorda used to call "Lasorda University." He used to say that the Holiday Inn was going to bronze our silverware because we ate there so much. We had a great time together. We really were like a family but not like the kids in *Sandlot*. We had different backgrounds, but we were a group. We didn't go places without each other. He made spring training fun, and for a lot of players, spring training is tedious and boring. You don't hear anybody talk about spring training being fun now. Players want to get there as late as possible and get out as fast as they can. I give Lasorda a lot of credit for making camp fun. There is no single blueprint for success, and Lasorda wasn't afraid to show people there was another way of getting things done.

Lasorda also had this incredible recall of people's names. He knew everybody's family and everybody's name in every family. It was ridiculous, and we couldn't believe that he could go a year or so without seeing a player's parent and then, "Hey, Joe, how you been?" It was uncanny and just one more reason why we considered him family to us. He cared so much about us. To have a person that dedicated and so close to you, it was rare. When they brought up the young players from the minor leagues, they promoted Lasorda from Triple A to coach third base in Los Angeles. Even then, we were still hanging out with him. When Lasorda became manager, that's when things changed and not in a bad way. It's just that we knew that he wasn't going to be able to devote as much time to us. It wouldn't be quite the same because he had bigger responsibilities. We accomplished an incredible amount of things together.

Lasorda, though, was complicated and he could be one stubborn son of a gun. Of all the years I spent with him and all the things I've done, the most upset he got with me was over something as insignificant as an autographed baseball. One of our game's unwritten customs is that the sweet spot of a baseball, where the seams are closest together, is reserved for the manager's signature. There was an event where we were both appearing, and attendees were randomly going from person to person to get signatures, depending on the lines. This was in recent years, and both of us were retired. When people got to me first and asked me to sign on the sweet spot, I signed on the sweet spot. Colin Gunderson, who was Lasorda's personal assistant, came over to me in the middle of the signing and said, "Tommy's really upset that you're signing on the sweet spot."

I started laughing and said, "I'm only signing the ball on the sweet spot because those people asked me to sign on the sweet spot. If Tommy's pissed, how do I know whether they're also going to get Tommy's autograph on this ball? It might be another ball. As long as they continue to ask me to sign on the sweet spot, I'll do it. And if they don't say, 'Sign on the sweet spot,' I won't."

Gunderson relayed that to Lasorda and came back to tell me that Lasorda wasn't happy with my answer. I said, "Well, I don't really care whether he's happy or not." Shortly after the event, we were in club executive Steve Shiffman's Dodger Stadium office, and Lasorda started airing me out, and Shiffman wanted to leave his own office because Lasorda was making such a scene. I told Shiffman, "You're not going anywhere. I'm not staying in this room alone with him." Lasorda was ranting, and finally I said, "Why don't you just knock it off? This is childish. It's a baseball. They asked me to sign on the sweet spot. Why don't you get some levity on this a little bit? It's not that I'm doing it intentionally to upset you. I'm doing it because they asked me to do it."

Finally, he calmed down and turned apologetic. And in the end, he put his arm on my shoulder and said, "Yeah, I don't want to have any issues with you. I don't want to have any issues with you ever." And that was the end of the sweet spot drama.

I used to tell him two different things when he got into that kind of mode. When he would say, "Penguin, didn't I tell you you're not supposed to sign on the sweet spot?"

And I would tell him, "Tommy, I'm one of those guys who got you into the Hall of Fame. So I'll sign that freaking baseball wherever I want." And then he would start laughing his ass off.

And the other one was: he'd say, "Penguin, you're not supposed to sign on the sweet spot. When did you ever manage?"

And I said, "Well, let me see. Oh yeah, I started in 1977." And that's when he started.

And so he'd say, "Oh, no, you didn't just do that. You didn't do that to me. So you're helping me manage? Is that what you're trying to tell me?"

I would try to make him laugh. I wasn't a clubhouse prankster. I wasn't a Jay Johnstone or Jerry Reuss type. But I wanted to nudge him out of that feeling of self-importance. He came around to understand I was just speaking the truth. A manager is only as good as his players. He started to realize he sometimes wasn't extending the credit to the players the way he should and, as time went on, he was doing more of that, and I felt good that he did. It made our relationship better.

Unfortunately with Lasorda, it was often either love or hate, and that makes me think about Bill Russell. For 25 years they were like father and son. But it went off the rails when Russell took over as manager after Lasorda had a heart attack in 1996. Lasorda groomed Russell for the job. But when the change was made, as the story goes, Russell was told by the front office not to let Lasorda influence his decisions. There was concern that Lasorda would be pulling the strings because he was so close to Russell. When that message was passed on to Lasorda, however, he felt that Russell had backstabbed him and Lasorda never forgave Russell. I don't know if that had anything to do with Russell and general manager Fred Claire being fired shortly after the 1997 Mike Piazza trade. But when Lasorda took over for Claire, the coaches closest to Russell—Mark Cresse, Reggie Smith, and Glenn Gregson—were fired. Lasorda never forgave Russell, and it continued until the day Lasorda died. It was visible to all of us. It was painful and hurtful. Russell played hard for Lasorda, helped Lasorda get into the Hall of Fame, and deserved better. Russell tried to patch it up, but Lasorda would have none of it. I know it really hurt Russell emotionally. I tried to intervene. Jimmy Campanis, Al's son, tried. The last time I tried, Lasorda said, "If you ever bring that up again, we won't be friends." It's one of the really sad chapters of my time with the Dodgers.

Lasorda never turned on me and, in fact, was my buffer with the front office because Campanis wasn't completely sold on me as the answer at third base. I felt like I spent a year longer in the minor leagues than I should have when he told me the job was mine to lose, but that wasn't the only problem I had with the front office. I was also the first Dodgers player to take the club to salary arbitration, baseball's process for having a third party determine a salary when the club and player can't reach a mutual agreement.

Maybe Campanis held that against me, but I never could get close to him. He never made me feel that he was on my side. For example, after my rookie season, Campanis thought I was overweight. He was wrong, I just had a stocky frame, but he saw it differently. To prove his point, he took me and Tommy John (who didn't exactly have a hard body) to the University of California at Davis because they had developed a test to determine your body fat content by submerging you in water. We flew to Sacramento and drove to Davis, and the two of us were lowered into this water tank and we had an apparatus attached and they told us to blow air into a tube connected to a monitor. The technicians read my result and said, "No, we've got to do it again. We've never had a result that low. There must be something wrong."

I had 5 percent body fat. We did it again, and again it was 5 percent. They insisted on a third test, and it came back the same. Campanis was just beside himself. He couldn't believe that Tommy John had 24 percent body fat, and I had 5 percent. Considering the Albuquerque fiasco in spring training, the arbitration result, and the weight thing, I couldn't help but feel Campanis really wasn't in my corner. Jimmy Campanis, Al's son and a former Dodgers player, told me that his dad really did like me as a player. I'm sure Jimmy truly believes that; he's always been straight with me about that stuff. It just really didn't feel that way.

To be fair to Al, he did give in to one of my requests. In 1974 I asked him for a separate hotel room on the road instead of sharing it with a roommate, which is the way it had been done for decades. He said nobody had asked for that. He said he'd think about it, but if he decided to do it, I'd have to pay the difference. Fine. When he got back to me, he not only said he would grant the request, but the club also would pay the difference. It led to single rooms on the road for everybody.

In contrast to my relationship with Campanis, my relationship with Lasorda was always strong, and that was a good thing. Lasorda could love you, but as the Russell fallout demonstrated, you wouldn't want Lasorda as an enemy. He'd make up his mind about an issue or a person, and there was no middle ground. He was the same way about addictions, and we had our share of those. Bob Welch and Steve Howe were the most visible cases. Lasorda felt that addictions were a sign of weakness—not illness—and he had no sympathy for those afflicted. Lasorda was opinionated about just about everything. He didn't waver. He loved that elite group of us. But there were a lot of people who were envious because he could make you or he could break you.

CHAPTER 4

THE INFIELD

June 23, 1973. It was a Saturday, Richard Nixon was president, Paul McCartney and Wings had the No. 1 song ("My Love"), and the Los Angeles Dodgers were in first place—three games ahead of the San Francisco Giants. We swept a doubleheader at a sold-out Dodger Stadium against the Cincinnati Reds, who would become known as the Big Red Machine. That was historic enough but would pale in comparison to the lineup Walt Alston posted for the nightcap. It included Steve Garvey at first base, Davey Lopes at second base, Bill Russell at shortstop, and me at third base. It was the first time the four of us started a game together as an infield unit, and we would remain that way with only an occasional day off for eight-and-a-half years, a major league record that won't ever be broken, in my opinion. We went on to win four pennants and a World Series together.

The planets aligned big time for that to happen. We had to be good enough, long enough. We had to have a management that embraced stability—even when it was known for developing young players and wasn't hesitant to promote them. Lopes was the oldest one of our infielders at 28 and Russell the youngest at 24. Three of us came out of the historic 1968 draft at a time when the big league club was still reeling from the retirement of Sandy Koufax after the 1966 World Series loss to the Baltimore Orioles. The timing was ideal for a foundational group to move in if it could sustain its level of performance—and we did for almost a decade. If we weren't the best infield of all time, we were the most successful. Every member was a multi-year All-Star, we appeared in more World Series than any infield, and we won a world championship. We won more games than any group of infielders in the history of the game. There's really no comparison because nobody even got halfway to what we did. For us each to stay relatively injury-free and play 150-plus games just about every single year while contending in just about every single year is an achievement that has nothing comparable.

Drafted out of Pittsburg, Kansas, Russell came into the organization first in 1966. The rest of us were products of Al Campanis' legendary draft of 1968, which ultimately produced 15 future major leaguers, 11 signing out at the draft, nine of which played for the Dodgers. Most drafts produce two or three big leaguers per club. Until 1965 the Dodgers could outfox, outspend, and overwhelm competitors for talent through diligent scouting and a vast farm system. To level the playing field, Major League Baseball implemented a draft system in 1965, and the Dodgers' results were mixed the first few seasons. Campanis needed a new approach and he borrowed one from professional football, which already had a draft in place. He spoke with Los Angeles Rams owner Dan Reeves and San Diego Chargers coach Sid Gillman, the latter referring him to Chargers director of personnel Al LoCasale. "LoCasale actually showed me how to draft," Campanis told *Baseball America*. "He explained the difference between drafting the best athlete or going for need. He showed us how to rank players on a scale of 100 based on fundamental skills. He took a neophyte and taught me how to approach a draft, and I think this helped us."

In that epic 1968 draft, the Dodgers landed six future All-Stars— Lopes, Bill Buckner, Tom Paciorek, Doyle Alexander, Garvey, and me—plus Geoff Zahn, Bobby Valentine, and Joe Ferguson, who each enjoyed lengthy MLB careers. It formed a nucleus that would pay off with four pennants and one World Series title from 1974 to 1981. For those who relate to Wins Above Replacement, according to *Baseball America*, the Dodgers' 1968 draft produced a WAR of 235.6 for those 11 players. Only the Boston Red Sox's 1983 draft comes within 50 of that.

Here's a fact that has been virtually forgotten about that 1968 draft: in the fifth round, the Dodgers selected Bill Seinsoth, a power-hitting first baseman and College World Series hero from USC. Seinsoth didn't sign in 1968, went back to USC, and was drafted again by the Dodgers in 1969. That time he went in the first round and signed for a $40,000 bonus. Management seemed to plug him in as the heir apparent at first base. I played with Seinsoth at Bakersfield that year and I believe he would have been the first baseman of our record-setting infield because he was a natural first baseman and left-handed hitter. After our season was over, Seinsoth offered to drive me back to Los Angeles, but our schedules weren't in synch, and I found another ride.

I never saw him again.

Seinsoth was killed in a car accident driving home, and to this day, I often wonder—and sometimes feel a little guilty—at how fate took Seinsoth and spared me. His coach at USC, Rod Dedeaux, was quoted in the *Los Angeles Times* as saying, "If Seinsoth had lived, there's a good chance that no one would have ever heard of Steve Garvey." I don't know about that, but as good as the Dodgers' 1968 draft was, it could have been even better.

Lopes was drafted in the second round of the January secondary phase, I was a third-rounder in the June phase, and Garvey was the 13th overall pick in the first round in June. My path was the most predictable. I was always a third baseman. Russell and Lopes were transplanted outfielders tutored in the intricacies of the middle infield by infield instructor extraordinaire Monty Basgall, who would later be rewarded as Tom Lasorda's bench coach. Garvey had a gifted bat but no defensive position because of an erratic arm and landed at first base after failed trials at third base and left field.

Third base had been a revolving door for the Dodgers for at least a decade, if not since Brooklyn. The media was obsessed with it, and each new tryout every spring training was reminded of it. There had been 42 other third basemen since the Dodgers came to L.A., starting with Dick Gray in 1958. That's a ridiculously high number, but I really didn't understand that history and wasn't worried about it. Once I was given that opportunity, I knew the job would be mine. I didn't feel like I broke some kind of voodoo spell and didn't necessarily take much satisfaction in stopping it. It's almost like I kind of expected it. I was very proud that I stabilized the position, but I thought it was a task I could handle in the first place. I never viewed it as too tall a mountain to climb. Playing third base was just another thing that I had to do. The media has a way of grabbing onto a narrative, and the "Dodgers' Black Hole at Third Base" was the headline. But I never got caught up in that. Third base was just my position. It's what I did, and if I played well over there, the Dodgers would be a better team. So the narrative turned into plugging a hole that had been nagging at them for years.

Garvey came from a Catholic family and grew up in Tampa, Florida. He was involved in all sports growing up, in particular football and baseball in high school, and had a scholarship to play both at Michigan State. His father was a bus driver for Greyhound who drove the Dodgers' bus during spring training. Garvey went to work with his dad when not in school and got to know the Dodgers back then, including some of the Boys of Summer. Garvey said his favorite player was Gil Hodges. So the

Garveys already had a connection with the Dodgers before Steve even became one. We had a lot of bus trips during spring training, and Garvey's dad was still going strong, still driving our bus. Like a lot of things with the Dodgers, the people who worked for them were treated like family. And we got to know Joe Garvey pretty well. He was a nice, friendly guy.

Although Steve also played football, his future was in baseball because he always could hit. He signed as a third baseman but had trouble throwing. Then they tried him in left field, but that didn't work. So eventually he wound up at first base. Technically speaking, first base was probably the last place that you go before the designated hitter came along. So Garvey was the last one of us in place, and actually it was the result of an (un)lucky break. Bill Buckner was going to play first base. Von Joshua was going to be the starting left fielder. But Joshua broke his wrist in spring training. Meanwhile, they needed a position for Garvey because they obviously liked his bat. So they went to Buck first and asked him if he would play left field, and Buck said he was good with it, and that opened up first base for Garvey. If Joshua doesn't get hurt, or if Buckner wouldn't have moved to the outfield, who knows what would have happened?

Garvey always hit and insisted on playing every game. We all wanted to play every game; that's why we lasted so long as a unit. It made things easy for Lasorda to make out the lineup. Garvey was productive at the plate, he became very good at fielding ground balls and digging out low throws from the other infielders, he was durable enough to set a league record for consecutive games played, and he crafted an extremely popular public image.

Nobody is a perfect player, and neither was Garvey. His throwing arm was erratic, and he knew it—to the point that he was reluctant to throw to other bases. That would come into play if our pitcher picked off a runner breaking to second base or on a grounder sending a runner from first base to second base. Sometimes he would just glove the ball and walk over to first base for an easy out rather than throwing to second base. If it wasn't a game changer, you just let it go. But the guys would get upset when it was the tying or winning run that was going down to second base uncontested. It was especially disconcerting to a pitcher who sets a ground ball—only to see a runner advance into scoring position. Lopes would give me that look of disgust. It was an irritant that led to at least one meeting with Alston. He said, "I totally understand. I agree with you guys. But here's the deal, here's how I see it: if you have him throw the ball down to second base, the ball's going into left field, and that's going to make the situation even worse. That way, we don't even get an out. For the time being, we're going to have to live with it. We're going to work on it, but we're going to have to live with it for the time being."

It didn't help that somehow Garvey kept winning Gold Glove Awards despite his limitations. It was attributed to a shoulder injury, and I guess that's true. You could say that maybe he should have worked on his throwing more. But I also understand that when you have a problem like that, sometimes it might be better just not to be reminded of it so much. Take a break from it. There are kind of two ways to go. I think Alston wanted to change it. I think he probably made an effort to change it. But it just wasn't going to happen because if Garvey threw the ball to second base and it went into the outfield, you knew that he wasn't going to throw down there anymore for quite some time. And yeah, he did make some throws, but his liability was his arm, and there was concern about it. As Alston said, it was just something we had to live with.

Garvey's greatest tool was his bat, and he put the ball in play, which is normally what you want a hitter to do. But we also had premier base stealers on base ahead of him, especially somebody like Lopes, who could steal bases successfully at such a high percentage. There were times when Lopes was really pissed because he was the kind of speed guy that you've got to let run. *If* you get an elite base stealer like that—Maury Wills, Lou Brock, Ricky Henderson, Ty Cobb or even Vince Coleman or Willie McGee—you've got to let these guys run when they take off so they get into scoring position because they rarely get caught. And if they get a big jump and the batter fouls a pitch off, you've wasted their energy.

Lopes was very athletic, and his asset was speed and quickness. He had a strong arm as well, having originated in the outfield with the speed to run down balls in the gaps. He and Russell were prototype center fielders because of their speed and strong arms. Lopes came from a large Portuguese family. He grew up in Rhode Island and got a scholarship to play basketball at Washburn University in Kansas. He was exactly the type of player the Dodgers targeted to change positions because his tools adapted around the diamond and he had the willingness to make the transition. Campanis used to talk fondly of moving players around the diamond, calling it "coconut snatching." He was particularly proud of the success enjoyed by Lopes, who quickly established himself as a player to be reckoned with. A talented base stealer, he created havoc for the opposition and served as our offensive catalyst atop the batting order. As a bonus, he was outspoken and would wear his feelings on his sleeve, which at that point in time was a good thing for us, a leadership skill. Part of that probably came from his time as a point guard in basketball because he was directing plays on the court. To bring out some of that leadership, he eventually was appointed captain of our team by Lasorda. Even though he was outspoken, we had a number of guys who were unofficial cocaptains, a nucleus of players I felt had leadership qualities and who were always in the mix, calling team meetings, speaking up when something went a little sideways.

I think Lopes was one of the top five second basemen in baseball in his time. Some compared him to Joe Morgan, the Reds Hall of Famer. Morgan was a great player on a great team and he had a lot of big bats driving him in with Johnny Bench, Tony Perez, George Foster, Ken Griffey, and even Dave Concepcion and Cesar Geronimo near the bottom of the order. Lopes doesn't get enough credit for being our version of Joe Morgan. When you look at all his stolen bases—twice more than 70—I can tell you that both of those years he was worn out. He was doing a lot of diving back into first base, and you may not think that takes a lot out of you, but if you dive three or four times back into the first base and then have guys fouling off pitches, you get gassed. It's another reason why I felt that Garvey and I were misplaced in the lineup with Garvey fourth and me fifth because I took walks, and Garvey didn't. I would let Lopes run. And I remember a conversation that we had when Russell and Lopes were both upset because they were trying to steal bases, and Garvey was fouling pitches off. I just told them if they're on base when I come up, run early. I'd much rather have you down there so I can drive you in.

Russell was a very good player in the clutch, which is an attribute a lot of players don't have. Pressure didn't seem to bother him. He was also a really good bad-ball hitter. What do I mean by that? He could handle pitches out of the strike zone, and a lot of hitters can't. He could especially hit fastballs up, often with two strikes, when you're in survival mode. Nowadays when pitchers get two strikes on a hitter, they like to end the at-bat with a high fastball and get the batter to chase because it's hard to catch up to high heat. But not for Russell. I remember an at-bat with him against Nolan Ryan, who threw a fastball above his letters, and nobody hit a high Ryan fastball. But Russell doubled down the left-field line. It was an at-bat that just stuck in my mind because it's not the kind of pitch that hitters would send down the left-field line. The best bad-ball hitter I remember was Manny Sanguillen of the Pittsburgh Pirates. It was impossible to throw a pitch far enough outside that he couldn't get to. There were pitches you not only couldn't believe he hit, but you also couldn't believe he swung at them. The joke on the scouting report was throw it down the middle. Russell wasn't quite that extreme, but he put tough pitches in play and he came up with the big hit many times.

There were those who said Russell didn't dive for balls, but I never bought into that. When you have a middle infielder that's going up the middle or going into the hole and they have to take two or three steps to dive for a ball, they've got a real good chance of messing themselves up. If it's the tying run, the winning run, and it's late in the game, I mean that takes on a different perspective. But asking a middle infielder to be diving all over the place is like asking an outfielder to run into the wall to try to make a play. That is really dicey out there. So if there is criticism of Russell for not diving for balls, that's like trying to tell me that the reason I'm not in the Hall of Fame is because I didn't steal bases. They didn't get me to be a track star. I'm not the guy who runs your 100-meter dash, right? Lopes is not the guy who you want to hit in the fourth spot, okay? I mean, it just makes sense.

Russell was as determined a player as I played with. In spring training during the first year or two, we were playing a game at Holman Stadium in Vero Beach. Russell was having a nightmare game. The first ball hit to him, he threw it away. Two innings later, there was a ground ball that just ate him up. He made a relay throw from the outfield and airmailed it to the backstop, and there was another ball he didn't catch. And the game was only about half over. I finally said to him, "Hey, don't you think it might be a good idea to call it a day? You're gonna wear this for a couple of days."

It's like a pitcher getting raked. Don't keep him out there all day to have to live through it. But he said, "I want to try to work it out right here."

He made another error, and I said, "Don't you want to take a break? Don't you want to get out of here? Just take your uniform off and just go home and just get this out of your mind."

He was like, "I'm okay." He said it's a tough day, but he'd be okay. He didn't back off on the field. None of us did. I give him a lot of credit.

The reason I think Basgall doesn't get enough credit for converting Lopes and Russell from the outfield to the infield is what I believe is a misperception about moving defensive players around the diamond. It's not as easy as people think. We are not interchangeable checker pieces. We have different histories, strengths, weaknesses, and skillsets. Changing positions is probably one of the toughest things to do in baseball, not one of the easiest. If you have a player who you're trying to convince to try something new and is unwilling to really get into it and work at it diligently, then it's best to not go there. When Paul Konerko was in the organization with Adrian Beltre, they had two really terrific prospects who were also third basemen—much like when Garvey and I were initially considered third basemen. Konerko was a little bit more advanced and older than Beltre at the time. Konerko was signed as a catcher, but he had a congenital hip problem. Squatting behind the plate wasn't going to work out. They didn't want to put him over at first base right away because that's the last place you want to go—no offense to the guys who played over there. But they tried to work him out at third base. I had a chance one spring to be there as a visiting instructor and work with him. I said, "So that I know that you're on top of this, that you are in this to get the best out of it, I want you to be able to recite the game back to me afterward."

And I told that to Glenn Hoffman, who was our minor league coordinator under farm director Charlie Blaney, and Hoffman said, "Oh my god, I've never heard anything like that."

And I said, "Well, this gives me an opportunity to see his concentration level, if he's into it. Because if he's out there just twiddling his thumbs, he won't be able to recite anything back. But if he's into it and understands that he needs to be aware of everything that's happening, he'll probably succeed."

One year they wanted Russell to switch-hit in order to take advantage of his running speed. It was the instructional league, and Russell was pinch-hitting left-handed against one of the Seattle Pilots' starters in Tempe, Arizona, where the Angels now train. I think he'd been at bat maybe a couple of times left-handed, and he hit a ball over the right-field scoreboard left-handed. I couldn't believe what just happened. He hit a ball over the scoreboard? Guys on their normal side can't do that. So, it started off pretty good. He was making good contact, having good swings, and I'm thinking, *This is working*. But he ran into some trouble. He was struggling to where it was affecting other aspects, including his right-handed hitting. It just kept getting worse. Instead of breaking him there, they backed off. The project was hurting him more than it could help him. Kudos for trying, but he went back to the right side and stayed there. It was asking a lot of Russell not only to move from the outfield to the infield, but also learn how to hit left-handed.

They didn't ask Lopes to switch-hit, just learn to play second base. Russell and Valentine were athletically the best shortstop types because they were the two fastest kids in camp. Lopes could run. Both Russell and Lopes bought into the conversion. They both had played basketball, so their footwork was good. They were up the middle, and I was at third. With Russell and Lopes, it was just a matter of convincing them.

You've got to have the young player buy into a switch. Otherwise, he's going to fight it, and it's going to be detrimental. It's just that he doesn't have the confidence. That's like trying to get me to be a catcher. I'm not going to be okay with that.

I look at the infield conversion of Russell and Lopes as being much more difficult than anything I had to do. When I was in the instructional league, they experimented with me defensively. They considered catching and second base and actually put me in the outfield for a game. I'd never played there before except when I was a kid. They put me in a game. There was a ball hit down the left-field line early in the game. I was able to go over and cut it off and threw out a guy at second base. I was thinking, *Wow, I didn't know I was going to be able to do that.* But then I'm thinking, *Why didn't you airmail it?* Because now they're going to think that maybe I can play left field, and I knew that I couldn't play left field. With the catching part, Basgall came to me with that. And I said, "Monty, look, if I can't play third base in the big leagues every day, then you can put me wherever you want. But until that happens, I want to concentrate on third."

One of our biggest assets as a unit was the familiarity that comes with repetition, and that point was driven home when it began to come to an end. When Lopes got hurt in the second half of 1981, Steve Sax was called up from Double A to play second base. Things I took for granted with Lopes I had to teach to Sax. For example, I told Saxy the same thing I told Ryne Sandberg when I joined the Chicago Cubs about my feeds from third base to second base. Defensively, my strength was my throwing accuracy. So I basically told them, "If we have a play that we can turn two, I'm going to try to always feed you to the inside of the bag, so when you come across, you're going to have that momentum toward first base. I'm going to lead you to the ball, and you're going to get out of the way of the runner as you throw. And on plays that we're just going to get a force play or I have to go down the line or if I dive for a ball and there's only a force-out possibility at second base, I'm always going to give it to you on the backside of the bag, and again you can get out of the way of the runner. And if I don't get it there, then it's on me. You can yell and scream at me all you want. But I'm going to make sure I give you that ball on the backside so you don't get killed over there." That's the kind of thing I wouldn't have to say to Lopes, but with Saxy and Ryno, that's the kind of stuff that you need to go through.

Nowadays players are shuttled in and out day after day, inning after inning. It's usually based on matchups and analytics, and I get it. But the counterargument was that we knew what to expect from each other and we made adjustments, taking into account our strengths and weaknesses. Now the players have cheat sheets they stuff into their caps or pockets that show the infielders and outfielders the tendencies of the hitters and how they will be pitched. We did a lot of that by memory. And we'd count on each other for help. I used to rag Russell when he'd miss giving me a pitch signal. He used to yell out "Penguin" or something like that when an off-speed pitch was coming because he could see the catcher's sign from shortstop that I couldn't see from third base. That really helped. When a right-handed pull hitter was up, I'd be ready for a ball down the line and I wanted to be maybe one step closer to that side if a guy's going to turn on it. And when he didn't give me a heads-up, I'm saying, "What the hell pitch was that?" And that is the kind of relationship we had. We were on top of things most all the time. In today's game you have all this information to process and different guys coming in and out. We became automatic. And then after a while, you just knew that we were in sync. You didn't have to worry; all you had to do was go out there and focus on your job. We were out there every single day for each other. I can't imagine if I was a manager today and you didn't know who's playing second base today or left field tomorrow. I think it's just a huge asset that we had that security above and beyond everybody else.

Of course, nothing lasts forever. As perfectly as the 1981 season ended, spring training that year began with the clock ticking, and we all heard it. We had been together a really long time and we had started to see a new group of young players knocking on the door because our farm system was very productive. The group of young players being groomed to replace us was probably the best group the farm system had produced since we had come up. We had two very talented young hitters, Mike Marshall and Greg Brock, who were primarily first basemen. They weren't just knocking on the door; they were tearing it off the hinges. But Garvey was a fixture at the position, and they can't all play there. Marshall won the Triple Crown in the Pacific Coast League in 1981 and was sent back to the minor leagues in 1982 because there was no place to play him in Los Angeles. Brock hit 44 home runs in the Pacific Coast League in 1982. Marshall could play in the outfield, which eventually he did. Sax was gunning for Lopes' job at second base. Dave Anderson was a first-round pick and the supposed heir apparent to Russell at shortstop. Candy Maldonado was a Puerto Rican outfielder drawing comparisons to Roberto Clemente. Pitchers Alejandro Pena and Tom Niedenfuer were called up after the 1981 strike and were ready for the big league staff, as was Ted Power. We couldn't keep these guys in Triple A forever. They'd done what they needed to do, and something had to happen. Pedro Guerrero, who shared the World Series MVP Award with me and Steve Yeager, was being talked about as the guy who would replace me at third base. If Guerrero could play third base, that would open up left field for Marshall, and Brock would take over first base for Garvey. They had a new wave of players ready to go, just like they did with us a decade earlier. It was evident that our time was running out.

It would have been a real shame if we hadn't been able to finally pull off a World Series in 1981—and not just because we had come so close so often. With the youth movement about to happen, this was probably our last chance. Campanis used to say it's better to trade them too early than too late, and the cut-off age for him was about 35. When Campanis traded Lopes shortly after we won the 1981 World Series, the writing was on the wall. There was chatter the entire year of 1982. Gossip from upstairs trickled down between the walls and into the clubhouse. We weren't supposed to hear it, but I think it was unintentionally intentional. And I completely understood because a decade earlier we were the young guys they had to make room for. It was kind of ironic actually. I didn't think that somebody was going to take my job. I felt like I had plenty left. And I proved that. I just felt that there was a decision that was being made that they were just going to move us out. And, really, how many more years would we have played together successfully while possibly shutting the door on these young kids having an opportunity? It was their time to play. We understood that, at least I did. But I was still hoping that there might be an opportunity for me to finish my career as a Dodger.

Once we won the World Series, it pretty much gave management license to turn over the roster and filter in the younger players. It began a few months after the World Series win when Lopes was unloaded to the Oakland A's for Lance Hudson, a minor leaguer who never reached the major leagues. That was a complete giveaway to open up second base for Sax, as Lopes would play six more seasons. Knowing that they wanted to move Guerrero to third base, I always thought I would be the first domino to fall. It was a total surprise to everybody that Russell outlasted all of us with the Dodgers. Simply because through all of the articles, we had been brainwashed into believing that he was going to be the first one to go. I felt if push came to shove, they could get enough in return for me. I did not think Garvey would leave. I didn't think they would push him out. He had a public-relations thing there that I thought made it a little bit difficult for them. So, I thought I was going to be the first one gone.

Turns out, I wasn't even the second to go. After the 1982 season— and a contentious few weeks of negotiations with the Dodgers—Garvey spurned the Cubs and signed a five-year free-agent contract with the San Diego Padres. Right after that, I had a one-on-one lunch with Peter O'Malley. He and I had a relationship that players don't usually have with owners, so we could talk about this. We didn't need to have the baseball executives. It was a personal thing. I think he felt that attachment to me. And I certainly felt that with him. And he put it all on the table, saying, "Listen, the plan is that Al and Tommy really want to move this new group in. I think it would be a good idea for you to move on and I'll help you as much as I can."

O'Malley said he didn't want me to be here and sit. He thought that even playing half the time would be painful for me. He said it was in my best interest and we should do it amicably. And I bought into it. Lopes had been gone a year, Garvey was gone, and then I was told that I was next. There wasn't a lot of time to absorb this because spring training was a month away. I really didn't want to uproot at that point in time. But I wasn't mad; I understood.

On January 19, 1983, I was traded to the Cubs for Dan Cataline and Vance Lovelace. Neither ever played for the Dodgers. I don't recall getting a call from Lasorda after that happened. But before I returned in May with the Cubs, O'Malley sent me a letter that he wanted to honor me with a Ron Cey Night. I was flattered. It was a big night and got a lot of play. We had a pregame ceremony that took about 20 minutes.

A lot of flattering things were said, and they gave me a bunch of gifts. It was all very much appreciated, and I felt really good about it.

I think we all wanted to be Dodgers for life. I know I did. I'm sure that Lopes wouldn't have minded that, nor Garvey. But Russell was the one who played his entire career with one team. Just a handful of guys get to do that. And he was the guy who the press felt was going to be the first one out.

• CHAPTER 5 •

POSTSEASONS

Before we won the 1981 World Series, some of my teammates mentioned that a few other teams presented miniature World Series trophies—in addition to the rings that have become synonymous with championships—to their players. If we won, our guys wanted them, too. And we planned on winning. So, I was asked to take it to owner Peter O'Malley. I told O'Malley the players would pay for the trophies; we just wanted his permission. He was overwhelmed it meant that much to us. He said he wished he had thought of that. And he said not to worry about the cost, that he would take care of it. O'Malley was very generous. He was thrilled we were able to do that on his watch.

So were we. It had been a long time coming, and very few players get as many chances as we had. Between 1974 and 1978, the Los Angeles Dodgers won three National League titles but lost the World Series each time. In 1974 we won 102 games in the regular season and topped the Cincinnati Reds, the Big Red Machine, which had overtaken the San Francisco Giants as our archrivals, by four games in our division. Getting past the Reds boosted our confidence for October because we had already eliminated what we considered to be our toughest competition. We were set to play the Pittsburgh Pirates for the pennant, even though Pittsburgh swept us in a pair of three-game series in June and August, then took two of three from us in September. The "experts" were a little bit skeptical of the way we matched up against Pittsburgh, but I don't think it weighed on us at all. We didn't bother to look back on it. We just felt that we were ready to go when playoff time came.

Don Sutton started Game One and shut them out 3–0 in spite of me. I had the worst playoff game in my career. I made two errors and didn't get a hit. And I was just a little bit upset about that. I was on center stage, and this is the time when you get some real important exposure and just went out and dropped a bomb. But we won. In my first at-bat in Game Two, the bases were loaded, and I had a chance to get that monkey off my back. And I fouled out. So, I was thinking, *This is not going well. I better get my act together here if we're going to win.* And I did, getting four hits by the game's end, including a home run and two doubles, and we won 5–2. We went home with two victories and were feeling pretty good. We missed a chance to sweep when Pittsburgh won Game Three 7–0, chasing Doug Rau in the first inning while Bruce Kison stuck it to us. We exploded in Game Four for a 12–1 win. Steve Garvey homered twice, helping put us into the World Series against the Oakland A's.

Once again, in Game One of the World Series, I made a throwing error and I don't remember throwing too many balls over first base in my career, but I guess the adrenaline and everything else was pumping pretty good, and it was totally uncharacteristic of me. From that point on, I had the longest-running streak of World Series games played at third base without making an error (22 games). We lost Game One by a 3–2 score, and Dodgers fans better remember it for the throw right fielder Joe Ferguson made from basically straight-away center field on a fly ball by Reggie Jackson. Ferguson cut in front of center fielder Jimmy Wynn and—with Sal Bando tagging and trying to score from third base—threw a missile to home plate. Bando and the ball arrived at the same time. No stranger to violent collisions, catcher Steve Yeager caught Ferguson's throw and hung on to the ball as Bando bowled him over. Wynn homered in the bottom of the ninth inning off reliever Rollie Fingers, but it wasn't enough.

Oakland's pitching staff was loaded with veterans—John "Blue Moon" Odom, Vida Blue, Catfish Hunter, Ken Holtzman. They were going for a World Series threepeat, and we played them tough but fell just a little bit short of what we needed. Losing, though, in five games was a little deceiving. It was far from a blowout, as three of our four losses were by one run, coincidentally all 3–2 scores. The clincher included a controversial break in the action before the bottom of the seventh inning as our left fielder, Bill Buckner, had the umpire ask the ground crew to clean up some garbage that had been thrown by fans onto the warning track. The fans had been giving it to Buckner because he had been quoted saying that only three players on the A's could have made the Dodgers' starting lineup. Mike Marshall was on the mound for us and he wasn't your average pitcher in any way, shape, or form. We used to call him "The Professor" because he had a PhD from Michigan State in kinesiology, and he thought he knew everything about how the body functioned. The delay to clean up the field took quite some time, but Marshall just stood on the mound with his hands on hips. He did nothing to stay loose, but he insisted everything was fine.

It was October obviously, and the stadium wasn't far from the bay and it was cold. Matter of fact, I felt uncomfortable the whole time up there. But Mike being Mike, he wouldn't throw any warm-up pitches during the delay, and it lasted a few minutes, maybe even three or four or five—definitely longer than a normal interruption. I asked him if he wanted to throw a few over to me at third base, but he said he was fine. When the outfield was clear and play was ready to resume, he declined to take the normal eight warm-up pitches. Marshall did unthinkable things that year for a reliever, appearing in 106 games and throwing 208 ⅓ innings, winning 15 games, and the Cy Young Award. But we all wondered what would have happened if he had taken the conventional warm-ups. What did happen without the warm-ups was Joe Rudi hit Marshall's first pitch of the inning for a home run. And it was literally a gamechanger. We ended up losing, but we beat ourselves a little bit. Buckner led off the top of the eighth inning against Fingers with a single that Bill North bobbled for an error as Buckner advanced to second base. Instead of stopping there, Buck tried for third and was thrown out—a cardinal sin with nobody out and trailing by a run. Fingers walked the next batter, Jimmy Wynn, but shut us down the rest of the way.

The A's deserved to win the series. That said, it was great for us to get our feet wet. Looking back on it now, I don't think we were intimidated; we just couldn't create anything offensively. There wasn't much action at all going on. Walt Alston came back in after the final game and closed the doors to the clubhouse. He said, "I just want to have your attention for a minute. This won't be long. I want you guys all to feel good about your year. It's been a great year. We won 102 games with a club that's up and coming. We have a terrific group of guys here. I want you to celebrate that if you can—more than the fact that I know you're disappointed about losing this series. But we're gonna have a chance to come back and do this again. And so that's really all I've got to say other than maybe we can get Garvey to throw the ball down to second base next year."

In 1975 and 1976, we ran into a steamroller with the Big Red Machine. They won 108 games and the division by 20 games in '75, they won 102 games and the division by 10 games in '76. They swept the Pirates for the '75 pennant and won the World Series against the Boston Red Sox. The next year they swept the Philadelphia Phillies and the Yankees to repeat as champs. They were the best team I ever faced. When 1977 came around, we were a little bit stronger. We needed a center fielder and got a good one from the Chicago Cubs in Rick Monday, who would deliver one of the biggest home runs in Los Angeles history a few years later. To get Monday and pitcher Mike Garman from the Cubs, the Dodgers traded my buddy, Buckner, along with Ivan DeJesus and Jeff Albert. We came out of the gate on fire. In April we finished the shortened month 17–3, and that's when I set a major league record for driving in the most runs in the month of April (29) in only 20 games. That's not only the biggest month in Dodgers history, but one of the best ever, according to Baseball-Reference.com, based on OPS (on-base percentage plus slugging percentage). We led the division by seven-and-a-half games by the end of April, and that catapulted us into a relatively easy regular season.

By mid-May we had a 12-game lead, and my focus kind of turned to be ready in October. And I finished the season horribly, going hitless in my last 31 at-bats, but Tommy Lasorda still left me in the lineup. The playoffs opened against the Phillies, and in Game One, we were down 5–1 in the bottom of the seventh inning against Steve Carlton, who I had hurt in the past. We loaded the bases, and I was up in this horrible slump. The count was 3–2, and it was a battle, lasting eight pitches, and I slugged a grand slam to tie the game. Unfortunately, the Phillies scored twice in the ninth for the win, but the rally lifted me and the offense. The next day Dusty Baker also hit a grand slam off Jim Lonborg, and we cruised to a 7–1 win as the series moved to Philadelphia. In Game Three our starter, Burt Hooton, was squeezed by plate umpire Harry Wendlestedt, whose strike zone became painfully small on borderline pitches. Hooton walked in three runs in the second inning. There was a big to-do about that. I was kind of thinking, *Are you really trying behind the plate? I'm filling up the strike zone, and you're calling everything a ball.* Hooton got affected by it. He was very, very, very upset for good reason. That was not easy to overcome, especially on this stage.

We began our comeback in the fourth inning when I doubled, and Baker singled me home to tie the game. The Phillies regained the lead 5–3 off Elias Sosa in the bottom of the eighth to set the scene for an unlikely comeback in the top of the ninth inning. With two out and nobody on base, 37-year-old pinch-hitter Vic Davalillo bunted for a single. Then 39-year-old pinch-hitter Manny Mota doubled on a ball that Greg Luzinski couldn't catch at the right-field fence. Mota's ball ticked off Luzinski's glove, and there was a lot of second-guessing that Danny Ozark, the Phillies' manager, should have replaced him on defense. The ball was catchable, and Luzinski didn't make that play. In all fairness, though, Mota's not supposed to hit that ball that far, right? He's really not. But he did. Phillies cutoff man Ted Sizemore, a former Dodgers infielder, dropped the throw as Davalillo scored, and Mota reached third. Davey Lopes then beat out a ground ball that deflected off third baseman Mike Schmidt and caromed right to shortstop Larry Bowa. The throw to first base by Bowa was bang-bang, and the umpire, Dutch Rennert, called Lopes safe. To this day, I still don't know what the right call was. And even in replay, it is really close. I will take Bowa's word that they got a little bit hosed on this. But that call was huge. The Phillies still could have escaped as they had Lopes picked off first base, but he wound up at third on Gene Garber's wild pickoff throw. Bill Russell singled up the middle to score Lopes, and we held on for a 7–6 win. We clinched the World Series berth with a 4–1 win in Game Four, as Tommy John outpitched Carlton in a rainstorm, and Baker smashed a two-run homer.

Because Veterans Stadium had artificial turf, they had the Zamboni out there vacuuming up the water. It was a game that shouldn't have been played—period. We had a ground-ball pitcher on wet turf, and you figured every grounder was going to shoot through you like a slip-and-slide. Even if you gloved the ball, it's soaking wet, and then you had to throw it accurately. But those guys didn't hit a ground ball hard. Otherwise, it could have been a disaster. They could have had 20 ground-ball singles or something, but we got through it and went to the World Series.

It opened in Yankee Stadium, and in Game One, Don Gullett started for the Yankees, and they won the opener while we didn't do much. Against Catfish Hunter in Game Two, I hit a two-run home run in the first inning to get us started, and that lit a fire. Yeager, Reggie Smith, and Garvey all homered, and we won 6–1. Hooton went all the way to tie the series. We went home feeling pretty good about it, but we lost Games Three and Four and just couldn't get any clutch hits. Facing elimination, Yeager and Smith homered, and we coasted to a 12–2 win in Game Five. We went back to Yankee Stadium for Game Six and took an early lead, but then Jackson, who had signed with the Yankees as a free agent, went off and hit three bombs off three different pitchers—Hooton, Sosa, and Charlie Hough. We were battling to tie the series at three games apiece, and instead this guy had a career World Series game. *Really? It had to happen right now?* It was kind of painful. You're just sitting there saying, "Geez, he's gonna hit another home run now?" It was kind of a helpless feeling when a guy's having that kind of game. Nothing you could do to change it, and the Yankees won the series in six games.

We ran away with the division in 1977, but 1978 was a different story. We had to battle the entire year. We were six games back in late June and didn't get into first place until late August during a series in San Francisco. We extended our lead to nine games in mid-September and held on to win the division by two-and-a-half games. Once again we played the Phillies for the pennant and once again we won three games to one. We just had a confidence about playing teams in the National League East. We felt that we were just better and that we'd already topped our toughest National League opponent, Cincinnati. No disrespect intended to the Phillies, Pirates, or Montreal Expos. They had great teams and great players, but we were that confident and we played that way against the Phillies.

We won Game One 9–5, as Garvey hit a pair of home runs, and Lopes and Yeager had one each in support of Bob Welch, the winning starting pitcher. Tommy John threw a four-hitter in Game Two for a 4–0 win, and we were in command. And just like the Pirates in '74, the Phillies were down to us 0–2, but they came out for Game Three pretty loose instead of being tight. They roughed up Sutton for seven runs en route to a 9–4 win, and we wrapped it up with a thrilling 4–3 win in 10 innings of Game Four. It was a heck of a game, a back-and-forth battle. I homered and doubled before reliever Tug McGraw walked me with two outs in the 10th. Baker hit a line drive to center fielder Garry Maddox, who dropped it and allowed me to go to second base. That brought up Bill Russell, and he got this big hit that dropped in front of Maddox, who couldn't field it cleanly. After watching the replay, I don't think there would have been a chance for him to throw me out anyway. On-deck hitter Jerry Grote was putting his arms up as I got to near home plate to let me know I could score standing up. I stomped on the plate because I knew that my run meant we were going back to the World Series. But I stomped on it a little too hard. And I felt it. And I'm thinking, *God, that would have been horrible if I got hurt scoring the winning run like that.* I saw their catcher, Bob Boone, walking back to his dugout with his head hanging down, and I felt for him. Having played against him in college, I knew him well and I completely understood. They got so close again, but we're going back to the World Series, not them. They would get it done two years later, but this was our time again.

And, again, it was the Yankees in the World Series. We won Game One in a blowout as Lopes homered twice and drove in five runs. Game Two was against Catfish, and I blasted a three-run home run with two outs in the sixth inning and drove in all four of our runs. Jackson drove in all of their runs, but we held on to win 4–3. We went to New York sky high. Things were in place, we were healthy and playing well. Then Ron Guidry shut us down in Game Three, and we lost 5–1. We were still in good shape and took a 3–0 lead in the fifth inning of Game Four on a three-run blast by Smith. In the sixth inning, Tommy John was on the mound cruising, and we were on the verge. Then things went haywire. With one out and two on, Jackson singled in a run. Lou Piniella hit a tailor-made double-play grounder to Russell, who stepped on second base and threw to first for what should have ended the inning. But Jackson stopped midway between first and second, intentionally stuck his hip out at Russell's throw, and deflected it into foul ground as a run scored. That play was the reason interference rules were written. But there was no instant replay back then. The first-base umpire was Frank Pulli of the National League, and the second-base umpire was Joe Brinkman of the American League. The umpires collaborated, but it wasn't much of a collaboration. In those days umpires rarely overruled each other. They had an unwritten code of ethics to stand together, not show each other up. The call wasn't overturned, and instead of a 3–1 lead, it was 3–2. The Yankees tied the game in the eighth on an RBI double by Thurman Munson off Terry Forster. That hurt badly. The game should have been over with, but instead we went extra innings.

With two outs and two on in the bottom of the 10th, Piniella walked us off with a single against Welch.

I believe we would have gone out the next day and clinched if we had won Game Four. But it left such a bitter taste with us. Even though we'd been in this position before, I just don't think we handled it very well psychologically. We hung on to it too long. We were back the next day for Game Five, but we had a hangover from Game Four. By the fourth inning, we were down 7–2. It was like, *Did you guys get out of bed yet? Did you wake up yet? Do you understand what's going on here? We're on the verge of seeing this thing evaporate and go in a different direction just like that.* And it hurt. We lost that game 12–2 and came out for Game Six flat as well, even though we were back home at Dodger Stadium in front of our fans. It didn't matter. We were deflated. Our bubble had burst, and we couldn't seem to keep that from happening. That was the most bitter disappointment in my career. That one game just destroyed our opportunity to bring a world championship back to Los Angeles. You can say we should have gotten over that better, but we didn't. I don't know if anybody can tell you how they will respond to adversity. You'd like to think you're able to calmly keep it together and move on, but that was a little bit extra. This was for all the marbles. It's not a game you could just walk away from and say, "We'll get 'em tomorrow." We didn't.

The next year, 1979, was the worst year we ever had, and it was almost like we didn't wake up from what happened in the 1978 World Series until midway through the year. It was a hangover that seemed to never end. You started to wonder if our time was up. We were in last place at the All-Star break. We had so many injuries, but it was also as bad a Dodgers baseball as you're going to see. But when we got healthy, even though we were way out of it, we played on pride and had the best record in the second half. That was what we were playing for. We were playing to get it back. We had no chance for postseason play, but we certainly didn't want to play the second half feeling sorry for ourselves and then go to spring training the next year trying to find it. Because when you have to wait through the winter after finishing poorly, you're going to have a feeling of anxiety. You've got to wait three or four months before you can even get after it. Instead, we came out of it and finished in third place, which felt a lot better than it sounds.

In 1980 we won 92 games, improving 13 wins from 1979. We were locked in a tight race with the Houston Astros from the end of April until the end of the season. The schedule had us finishing up with a three-game series against the Astros at home, and we went into it trailing Houston by three games. We swept the series, and I homered in the eighth inning of the third game off Frank LaCorte to give us a 4–3 win and force a one-game playoff.

While everybody was pretty ecstatic about that home run and the victory, nobody realized that earlier in the at-bat I fouled a pitch off my left foot, and it felt like I'd been run over by a truck. I went home that night and had ice on my foot, and it wasn't responding. Ice and I usually got along really well. (Insert your own penguin joke here.) But at 2:00 in the morning, my foot was throbbing. I called the Kerlan-Jobe Clinic emergency number and asked when Centinela Hospital would open because I needed an X-ray. They told me I had to wait until 6:00 AM. I showed up, and they took an X-ray and then used a long syringe to drain fluid from both sides of my ankle. They sucked all this crap out of there and then they filled it back up with anti-inflammatory drugs. I got to Dodger Stadium around 9:00 in the morning, and there was hardly anybody there. I limped up the ramp in the players' parking lot and couldn't put any weight on my foot, and when I limped into the clubhouse, everybody's jaws dropped. It's Game 163, and there's no way I could play. Lasorda gave the start to Dave Goltz instead of recent call-up/rookie sensation Fernando Valenzuela, which became a heated second-guess topic when Goltz lasted only three innings in a 7–1 loss that ended our season.

With 1981 on the horizon, we knew time was running out. In spring training Lopes came out of nowhere and proclaimed that if we stayed healthy, we were going to win it all. I could just see that comment getting posted on bulletin boards in every opposing clubhouse. But I couldn't argue with what he said because I kind of felt the same way. We were due, and it was time to get this done. The window was closing from an age standpoint. Management was preparing to move us out. It's something you're not supposed to hear, but we did. We were in our mid-30s, and Lopes was even a little older. He understood. We all did.

Coincidentally, there also was a labor war brewing. Realizing the impact of free agency, the owners wanted to win back leverage over the players. Ultimately, there would be a 50-day strike in the middle of the season. Leading up to that, we didn't know if there would be a stoppage or not, but we figured we better be in first place just in case. We barely were—by half a game—when play stopped. Cincinnati got robbed because the strike settlement guaranteed that the team in first place at the time of the strike—us—earned an automatic playoff spot. But we didn't know that going in. We certainly didn't know it would be ruled that way. We just said thank you very much. Winning the first half and a postseason berth gave us the opportunity to return after the settlement and not feel the pressure to play all out. What we did was play hard but at our pace. If we needed a day off, we took it. Cincinnati argued that because it had the best overall record that it deserved to be in the playoffs. I would have felt the same way.

But we were in, and the first round was a best-of-five series against the Astros, who won the second half of the season. I say "we" were in, but I was out. In September, Giants pitcher Tom Griffin hit me with a pitch that broke a bone in my left arm. I had to do a lot of self-healing. I spoke to my arm quite a bit about being ready in three weeks for the next series, while I kept my fingers crossed that we would get past the Astros. When the cast came off, my arm had atrophied. The minor league season was over, so there were no rehab games to work myself back into playing shape. They didn't have year-round programs in place like they do now. If you have a player needing game action in October now, they'll create something at their training sites in Arizona or Florida. Back then, I was on my own. When the cast came off, I was sore. My range of motion was limited. Meanwhile, our offense scored one run in the first two games against the Astros. Both were losses, and we were facing three consecutive elimination games. It was looking like even if I was ready for the next round, there wouldn't be a next round for us. But the series moved to Dodger Stadium, and our pitchers stepped up. Hooton won Game Three 6–1. Valenzuela outdueled Vern Ruhle 2–1 in Game Four, and Jerry Reuss threw a shutout to beat Nolan Ryan in Game Five to earn the right to play the Expos, who beat the defending champion Phillies.

I still needed to get the cast off my arm and be cleared to return for the series with Montreal. I went to the clinic to see Dr. Frank Jobe, our team doctor and the creator of the Tommy John surgery. Walking down the hall of the clinic, I reached the office of Jobe's partner and the Los Angeles Rams team surgeon, Dr. Robert Kerlan. The door was open, and I poked my head inside, waved my casted arm at him, and said, "This is coming off today." It was a statement, not a question.

Kerlan responded, "I hope you're right." The X-ray confirmed the break had healed, so everything was looking good, but I still hadn't played a game in five weeks. Ready or not, I would play.

Everybody remembers how we won the series—on Monday's dramatic home run—but a lot of people forget Hooton was named series MVP. Hooton took a shutout into the eighth inning of Game One, a 5–1 win, and allowed one unearned run into the eighth inning of Game Four, a 7–1 win that set up the decisive Game Five and Monday's heroics. If Hooton didn't win those two games, we probably don't get past the Expos. I went 2-for-4 with a double in my first at-bat in Game One, my first game back after breaking my arm. I drove in a run in Game Three in Montreal and had a pair of hits in Hooton's Game Four win, which tied the series. After a one-day postponement for cold weather, Valenzuela got the ball for Game Four.

The temperature was in the low 40s. When the ball comes off the bat in that weather, everything stings. The sound was a thud rather than a crack. I didn't think anybody would hit a ball out of that ballpark, especially where Monday hit his in right-center. Valenzuela gave up one run in the first inning on a ground-out and came within one out of a complete game. We tied the game in the fifth inning on Valenzuela's RBI ground-out. The rest of the game, the temperature continued to fall toward freezing, and you could sense the tension, as one mistake could determine who goes to the World Series. In the bottom of the eighth inning, Montreal pinch-hit for starting pitcher Ray Burris, and for the ninth inning, manager Jim Fanning brought in Steve Rogers, the Expos' ace starter. With two out and a 3–1 count, Monday launched his huge home run. Valenzuela got two quick outs and then walked Gary Carter and Larry Parrish. So Lasorda brought in Welch to get Jerry White on a grounder, and we were back in the World Series against the Yankees again.

Because of the playoff postponement, there was no travel day. We beat the Expos on Monday and opened the World Series on Tuesday in Yankee Stadium. There was no time to celebrate a pennant. New York jumped out to a 5–0 lead and won the opener, chasing starter Reuss in the third inning. Tommy John, our former teammate, and Rich Gossage combined on a shutout win in Game Two, and we were right back in an 0–2 hole. That should never be considered a good thing, but we came back from the same deficit to beat the Astros and Expos, so maybe that's just how we we're going to do it. In Game Three at Dodger Stadium, we put runners on first and third with nobody out in the first inning and we had Baker, Garvey, and me coming up. Baker popped out. Garvey struck out. I faced Dave Righetti, a rookie who pitched really well that season. I was in a battle with him, just missing a home run foul, and with the eighth pitch of the at-bat, I launched one, and we had a three-run lead. To their credit the Yankees battled back and actually took the lead on home runs by Bob Watson and Rick Cerone. Valenzuela wasn't sharp, but he was gutsy. He threw a 149-pitch complete game; Lasorda wasn't going to take him out.

We took a one-run lead in the fifth inning, and they opened the top of the eighth with singles by Aurelio Rodriguez and Larry Milbourne. With pitcher Rudy May's spot due up, Yankees manager Bob Lemon sent pinch-hitter Bobby Murcer up to bunt the runners over. Murcer bunted the first pitch into the air up the third-base line. I got a good jump, made a diving catch into foul ground, and recovered to throw across the infield to double up Milbourne with Lopes covering first base. For all of the defensive plays I made over my career, that one is probably best remembered. Willie Randolph followed and hit me a ground ball, and I tagged the runner to get us out of the inning, and we got a huge win after losing the first two games. Games Four and Five were also one-run wins, as we turned the series around. We were down 4–0 in Game Four after our starter, Welch, was lifted in the first inning after not getting a batter out. But Lopes, Jay Johnstone, and I drove in two runs each—Johnstone's came on a pinch-hit homer—and the bullpen kept us in it.

We won Game Five, but I wasn't around to see the finish. That's the game that Gossage beaned me in the head and left me with a ringing concussion. Pedro Guerrero and Yeager had homered back to back in the bottom of the seventh inning to give us a 2–1 lead. With two outs in the bottom of the eighth, Gossage threw an 0–1 fastball, and the ball just disappeared on me. I kind of ducked down, and it caught the bill of the helmet. I'm still not sure where the helmet ended up. I heard it one-hopped the first-base dugout. On the replay it looked like it went backward. It went flying, I know that. And I went down for quite a while. They finally got me up and walked me off the field and into the club-house and put an ice turban on my head. Lemon and Goose came over to check on me after the game. I'd known Goose for a while and I never believed he was trying to hit me. I never thought it was intentional, but I was happy they came over. We won the game 2–1, and an ambulance picked me up outside the dugout afterward. I had a CAT scan and MRI and got through those and went home.

The next day the team left for New York, and I went back to Centinela Hospital. After more tests I was cleared to fly and boarded a plane to rejoin the team in New York. (There were no concussion protocols back then.) I got to the team hotel at 1:00 or 2:00 in the morning. Lasorda and Jimmy the Greek (a Las Vegas bookmaker-turned-sportscaster) were in the lobby holding court. I walked in, and everybody scattered as Lasorda came over and wanted to know if I was playing the next day. I told him we'll have to wait and see. The next day I was still in a fog and had no idea whether I would play, but I didn't have to make that call. I got a break when the game was cancelled because of bad weather. It gave me another day to rest, which made a big difference. I went out early the next day, but instead of heading straight for the ballpark, I took a cab and rode through Central Park just for the calming effect. It was a relaxing ride through minimal traffic, and then I went to the ballpark and started my regimen before I could clear myself. I had to run, take grounders, hit. I did it all with no ill effects. What was really interesting—and unforgettable—were the people in the stadium. While I was on the field early, Yankees fans started cheering for me. It was kind of cool and classy.

Lasorda arrived and he started following me around like a shadow dog. Everywhere I went, he'd ask how I was feeling. I took ground balls and batting practice, trying to get used to a new helmet with a protective flap. He showed me the lineup with nobody listed in the fourth spot. Finally, I told him to go inside and leave me alone. Fortunately, this wasn't like Tony Conigliaro or Dickie Thon, who suffered more horrifying beanings. Nothing got smashed or fractured. It was just a matter of getting back on the horse. I headed back into that dungeon of a clubhouse, and a ton of reporters were waiting. I poked my head in and said I was good to go, and Lasorda wrote my name in the lineup.

The Game Six matchup was Hooton for us and Tommy John for them. On the first pitch I saw in the first inning since the beaning, I singled. In the fifth inning, I singled home Lopes on a ball that took a funny hop to elude Randolph, and we took the lead. Baker singled me to third, and while running, I started feeling a little dizzy. Guerrero then tripled, so I could walk home, and we ended that inning with a 4–1 lead. I went out to my defensive position for the next half inning, and Jerry Mumphrey hit me a little humpback liner, and it came at me like a fuzzy tennis ball. When the inning ended, I told Lasorda I needed to come out of the game. Things were a little off, and I didn't want things to be on me if something went sideways. I didn't want to be stubborn and not know when enough's enough. If there had been a game the next day, I could have played. Fortunately, we won the game 9–2 and thus the series. Steve Howe, our closer, pitched the final three-and-two-thirds innings (that's what closers did back then), and center fielder Ken Landreaux caught Watson's fly ball for the final out.

Finally, it was dogpile time—or as close to it as we did those days. We had completed this monumental achievement that had been eluding us for nearly a decade. It gave us a great feeling of accomplishment to do it with the infield still intact. It turned out that this was the last game we would play as a unit. The first four hitters in the lineup were the four infielders. What historical symmetry! We also had the 30-homer foursome—me, Baker, Smith, and Garvey—intact. Now we had it all. If we hadn't done that, the story would have been written quite differently. It was Lasorda's first world championship as manager. We now joined all the other great Dodgers teams that came before us and the respect that goes with it. The icing on the cake was the World Series Most Valuable Player Award, which I shared with Yeager and Guerrero. That's indicative of how this was truly a team victory.

And the icing for the whole organization was the parade. I'm sorry our current players who won a few of years ago during COVID-19 didn't get that parade. It was really special. We were on a big float, going right down the center of L.A., and ended up at city hall. It was nuts. Fans were running up to the floats, cheering and yelling. I had an opportunity to speak at city hall. It was a great thrill for all of us to experience. It's one of the reasons why you play this game for as long as you do. It's for that moment.

Every kid who has ever played this game has wanted to win a World Series. It was one of those sandlot moments going back into your childhood, playing in the street, playing Little League. The dream of being in that moment, finally being recognized. And to walk away with the MVP was like, *Really, I get this, too?* Individual recognition is nice, but mostly it was about cementing our own legacy. To represent a franchise with all the storied players and teams in the past was just a major accomplishment. There would have been a hole had we not finished the deal. There were years that I had that I wasn't happy with the overall results, knowing I should have done better. But when you win, it makes everybody happy. And when you lose, it makes everybody grumpy.

• CHAPTER 6 •

FROM JACKIE ROBINSON TO FERNANDOMANIA

I wish I had met Jackie Robinson. He didn't visit Dodgertown in my early spring trainings and then tragically died in 1972. As enjoyable and productive as my spring training sessions in Florida were, it also provided a glimpse at what Robinson must have dealt with while breaking baseball's color barrier. My first spring in Vero Beach, Florida, was 1969, and segregation was still a thing in the Deep South.

The late Don Newcombe, one of Robinson's teammates who became a Dodgers executive, was our link to Robinson and what the African American player went through back then. I came away from my conversations with Newcombe with an understanding of how delicate the process was for Robinson and the Dodgers to break the color barrier, how critical it was for Branch Rickey to pick the right person in Robinson, and how the African American community back then was just as fearful of the repercussions if Robinson failed as they were excited for his chance to succeed. If Robinson failed, it would be a long time before somebody else would get that opportunity.

Of course, the success was historic, and the Los Angeles Dodgers have continued those trailblazing ways. They were early in the search for talent in the Caribbean, establishing the first full-fledged training complex in the Dominican Republic. Campo Las Palmas was the vision of general manager Al Campanis and constructed in the early 1980s by his main man on the islands, Ralph Avila, the father of former Detroit Tigers general manager Al Avila and grandfather of catcher Alex Avila. But three decades earlier, Campanis discovered and signed future Hall of Famer and Puerto Rican Roberto Clemente, though the Dodgers lost him in the Rule 5 draft to the Pittsburgh Pirates.

The Dodgers also played a leading role in opening up the Pacific Rim with the signing of Japanese free-agent pitcher Hideo Nomo, who was Rookie of the Year in 1995 and added 123 Major League Baseball wins to the 156 he accumulated in Japan. The Dodgers triggered an influx of South Koreans to MLB with the signing of Chan Ho Park, who won double digits for the Dodgers five consecutive seasons. Left-hander Hong-Chih Kuo overcame two Tommy John surgeries and the yips (a sudden inability to throw accurately) to become the first prominent Taiwanese player in MLB. The Dodgers continue to hold clinics in Australia and Europe, forever searching for the best talent on the planet.

That wanderlust led the Dodgers to their most rewarding international signing in 1979. Campanis shared credit with legendary scout Mike Brito for the acquisition of the teenager from Etchohuaquila, Navojoa, Sonora, Mexico. They purchased the barrel-chested left-handed pitcher from the Mexican League for $120,000, outbidding the New York Yankees, among others. Fernando Valenzuela went on to help us win a World Series and launch a cultural revolution in our sport.

I first met Valenzuela when he was called up from Double A San Antonio during our stretch run in 1980. He wasn't in big league spring training camp because he wasn't on the major league roster yet, an indication that even management didn't foresee his meteoric rise. At the time, I just heard that there was this 19-year-old Mexican pitcher who they were very high on, had a pretty good season at San Antonio, and might be a helpful arm down the stretch. He looked very young, not exactly a physical specimen or a flamethrower, but he could fool hitters with a screwball, a pitch he learned from teammate Bobby Castillo. We also knew that he had a very sheltered background after an upbringing in a very small town.

Beyond that, we didn't know much about Valenzuela. But it was no secret that organization owner Walter O'Malley had long dreamed of having a fellow countryman, whom Mexican fans in Los Angeles could latch onto as their own. It was the one missing piece to his master planned move to Los Angeles, where we had such a large Hispanic population from which to draw. At that point that segment of the population had been largely untapped. And with Valenzuela it finally happened. Even before Fernandomania, Valenzuela was a sensation on the mound as soon as he arrived. He didn't allow an earned run in his 20 relief innings of that 1980 stretch run. Even though we barely missed the playoffs that year, those innings got his feet wet in big league surroundings and bolstered his confidence. The way he pitched in 1980, you knew he was going to be in the plans for the future.

At the time, Valenzuela spoke no English, and I think the best thing that happened to him was having our Spanish broadcaster and eventual Hall of Famer, Jaime Jarrin, as his interpreter. Jarrin has been with the Dodgers more than 60 years. He's been the Spanish voice of the team, the Spanish Vin Scully, if you will. And it was brilliant putting him in the role of Valenzuela's interpreter because having him in the middle just took a lot of pressure off Valenzuela. It gave Valenzuela the opportunity to kind of ease into this situation, which commanded so much attention that was unlike anything he had before in his life. When you throw a teenager with a sheltered background into that, it would have been absolutely overwhelming had he been on his own. I know I wouldn't have been ready for it at 18 or 19. So the *No hablo ingles* response was a very comforting and strategic move for him. I'm sure he was overwhelmed daily trying to deal with a world he knew nothing about aside from the baseball. So off the field, Valenzuela had that help.

In the clubhouse Valenzuela was very shy in the beginning. It was hard to communicate with him. We didn't have dedicated interpreters like they do now, and Jarrin was around only for the media. You'd grab a bilingual teammate or coach like Manny Mota to translate if you needed to get a point across. Otherwise, there wasn't a lot of clubhouse chatter with him. He was quiet, and we sort of left him alone because we didn't want to make him feel uncomfortable about his difficulties speaking our language. At least, that was what I tried to do. I didn't want to pressure him into communicating if he felt uncomfortable.

We all know what Valenzuela did in 1981, but when we got to spring training, nobody could have predicted that. In fact, it was a stretch to even envision Valenzuela cracking the starting rotation. We were loaded, to be honest. In 1980 we had five pitchers who started at least 32 games, and four of them were coming back in 1981—Jerry Reuss, Bob Welch, Burt Hooton, and Dave Goltz. Don Sutton left to go to the Houston Astros, but we also had Rick Sutcliffe. Valenzuela would have been battling just to get into that rotation. But Reuss went down with a strained calf in the workout the day before the season opener, Lasorda gave the ball to Valenzuela, and the rest is baseball history. It was like a Lou Gehrig/Wally Pipp story.

He seized the opportunity and had as great a start to a season as anyone ever: eight complete games, five of them shutouts. It was like Little League or video game stuff—except it's happening to a kid in the major leagues on a team that's expected to go to the World Series. He ended up winning the Cy Young and Rookie of the Year. Valenzuela showed the previous year he was ready for the major leagues, but nobody expected this. And remember: back then you didn't get force-fed the way they do today. It was a methodical progression through the farm system for most players with a year at each minor league level. When you came up through our system, you had to prove that you could play at each level and then hope that you were good enough to get an opportunity to play in the big leagues. But with Valenzuela they kind of rushed him through it because he answered every bell. We all saw how it turned out, but I really don't think even management intended to throw him into the fire like that. I'm laughing at it now; it seems so crazy what happened. By comparison, you look at what they did with Julio Urias, who in his early years was compared to Valenzuela because he's also from Mexico and also left-handed. But they babied Urias. They almost spoon-fed him step by step.

By today's standards and maybe even 1980s standards, Valenzuela was overused, and Lasorda got some heat for that. Lasorda was notorious for sticking with his pitchers, and certainly Valenzuela fit that bill. Pitch counts didn't show up in box scores until 1988, but even that late in his Dodgers tenure, Valenzuela had a 150-pitch complete game. I'm sure he had many starts with more pitches than that earlier in his career. Lasorda was an old-school manager, and his argument was that when he gave the ball to Valenzuela, he wasn't thinking about relieving him. Valenzuela was a workhorse. They didn't have analytics and metrics and data illustrating what opponents do the third time through a batting order—a popular data point these days. Lasorda let Valenzuela pitch until he got into a lot of trouble. And it probably led to his 1988 shoulder injury and took years off his career, but it also probably helped him set records and win awards and a ring. It was like with Sandy Koufax or Don Drysdale. When it was their day to pitch, it was their game—win or lose. They pitched until they couldn't get guys out. I mean, Koufax had 27 complete games each of his last two seasons. Today there might not be 27 complete games pitched in an entire league. So, Valenzuela was a throwback to the old type of pitcher. I think it was pretty clear the first couple of weeks of the season that Valenzuela had to be part of our rotation, and we would have to make room for him or push somebody else out. When you have a player that outperforms, then you have to find a way to get him in there, no matter his age or lack of experience, and he deserved it. And, bam, here came Fernandomania. I mean, the kid was not just winning games, but he also was pitching phenomenally and historically.

Was Fernandomania a distraction? You'd have to say it was, but it wasn't necessarily a negative one. It was a positive one. There was so much media converging on the clubhouse and on the field on days that he would pitch that it was chaotic. Morganna "the Kissing Bandit" ran onto the field to plant one on the kid. Fans worshipped him. And I want to give Valenzuela as much credit as I can, but we'd already drawn three million people, okay? No doubt he put even more people in the seats, especially on the road. But you have to give credit to the other people who were there before he was. Valenzuela was such a likeable guy. There wasn't any kind of jealousy or friction. None at all. We were already a good team, and he was the one who made it better. It was kind of funny in a sense because it kind of took some of the pressure off the rest of us. Everybody's following the kid around. So we didn't have to be distracted by some of the stuff that would normally go on. And I don't mean distraction in a negative way. But back then we didn't have the security rules in place that exist today. The media was free to roam the clubhouse and even the training room. They pretty much had all access while we had no privacy. The media could conduct interviews while we were taking batting practice, and believe me: that can be distracting when you're actually in the batter's box. But when they were in the dugout interviewing Valenzuela instead of coming up to us around the batting cage or BP, it was a little bit of a relief. And Jarrin was really good at conducting the press conferences and shutting it down so Valenzuela could get back to work, and the media could move on to the rest of us.

I always thought Valenzuela was a good guy. One time when Valenzuela was having a tough outing, I got the signal from the dugout to talk to him. I knew that I was going to take a slow walk to the mound, and Mike Scioscia was catching, so I kind of walked a little bit toward Scioscia first. Scioscia spoke enough baseball Spanish that he could get any message across to Valenzuela. And I told Scioscia that I thought he should tell Valenzuela that it's time for a taco and cerveza, and he started laughing.

Ron Perranoski, our pitching coach, probably didn't get enough credit for preparing Valenzuela to face hitters he knew very little about. This was long before the Internet and YouTube. Analytics was something taught at MIT but wasn't part of baseball. Breaking down opponents was done by the pitching coach with an assist from the advance scout. It seems archaic by today's standards, but it's pretty much all Valenzuela had. Even today, the pitching coach probably has the toughest job on the team because he's got to have a handle on 12, 13, 14 pitchers and he has to have a real understanding of each one. I thought our pitching coaches had a relationship with the pitchers that was a little bit more personal than maybe just business. They knew when a guy would be honest with him when asked if he was still able to pitch. Perry or Red Adams, our previous pitching coach, would go back to Lasorda or Walt Alston with the information that would be used to manage the game. Fortunately for us, we had a starting rotation that pretty much went out and did its job at a very, very high level most of the time. If you look back on our ERAs during those 10 years that I was there, you will find that two years our staff was under 3.00. Now there aren't guys in the top 10 in MLB under 3.00, and we had a whole staff. Our pitching staff was essential to our success.

No doubt Valenzuela and any foreign player coming into the major leagues have cultural obstacles to overcome that I didn't face. Some people then wonder why so many major leaguers originate on the islands in the Caribbean, and I think there's a logical explanation. Kids from places like Mexico and Puerto Rico and the Dominican Republic are simply playing more baseball than we do now. It's about repetition. When I was a kid, we played stickball—even if all you did was hit a rock—it still refined your hand-eye coordination. Kids from the islands are very advanced for their age, whether it's hitting or fielding. As a kid I used to throw balls on the roof and wait for them to roll down, and that helped me learn how to catch fly balls. I would throw balls off a wall or a porch step, and that helped me learn how to field ground balls. I imagine a kid like Valenzuela was playing ball every single day growing up often against older kids and even grown men. So that's my explanation of it. Some in the media speculated that Valenzuela was older than his reported age because he seemed too advanced from a baseball perspective. But to those of us inside the clubhouse, Valenzuela seemed really young.

Similar to Robinson opening the game for African Americans, Valenzuela's success paved the way for greater international participation, and in 1995 Nomo arrived from Japan. Although baseball had been played in Japan for decades, free-agent restrictions kept almost all native players at home. Nomo bravely challenged those rules, and the Dodgers provided him the perfect major league landing spot. Two decades earlier, I remember the Tokyo Giants being invited to train with us at Dodgertown, which was very much in keeping with Walter and Peter O'Malley's mission to grow the game internationally. I wouldn't equate Nomomania to Fernandomania, but it was a real thing. When Nomo came over, along came literally hundreds of Japanese media. And at that time, unlike Valenzuela with our already existing Hispanic audience, we really didn't have much of a Japanese following to speak of. But ever since Nomo, our Japanese fanbase has steadily grown. You can see it in the faces of the crowds at Dodger Stadium and the sponsorships from Japanese beer to tires and autos. It's sort of amazing even today to think about it, but when Nomo would start, those games would be televised back to Japan, and because of the time difference, they would be shown live in the early morning hours there, but the ratings were still through the roof. When Nomo was on the mound, it was a holiday in Japan and a circus at Dodger Stadium, a lot like the Valenzuela days. And it was really exciting to see more people getting involved in Dodgers baseball, people that we hadn't seen in the stands before.

Nomo was followed from Japan to the Dodgers by other impact pitchers like Kaz Ishii, Takashi Saito, Hiroki Kuroda, and Kenta Maeda. The appeal of Dodgers baseball led to lucrative sponsorships from Japanese companies and, accidentally, a sort of cottage industry for Lasorda, who would visit Japan multiple times a year to court high-rolling sponsors in his role as a special advisor to the owner. He used to tell me, "Penguin, you gotta come on one of these trips to Japan with me. They never run out of sushi."

He loved it, and they treated him rather well, and all of that stemmed from Nomo's success. Again, like Robinson, if Nomo failed, who knows how that plays out? A couple years after Nomo, the Dodgers signed Park out of Korea, and that opened up another country and another pipeline of players.

Probably more than any club, the Dodgers have done a really good job—for lack of a better term—of beating the bushes for talent. We've selected and secured a type of player and person who comes from another country and adjusts to our game and our city. Los Angeles is a potpourri of cultures, a melting pot of people, and it can still be a tough place to play. So if you succeed there, then you're probably going to be okay with all the pressure and everything else that goes with it. Playing in L.A. prepared Nomo for Boston and Kuroda for New York.

I've been asked if foreign players faced resentment from American players as a threat to their job security. Baseball is a merit-based profession where you get what you earn. It doesn't matter whether you're 6' tall or 5'5," or 260 pounds or 160 pounds, if you're Black or White, or Korean or Japanese or whatever. If you win the spot, it's going to be your job. And that's the way it should be.

That brings us back to Robinson. Nobody could criticize his talent, his drive, his work ethic, or his results. He was a great player, a difference maker. Curiously, I don't remember as much talk about Robinson's impact when I was a young player as there is today. I think it was taken for granted by all of us back then. It's not taken for granted now. Baseball seemed to realize it needed to revisit this achievement and recognize its magnitude. It should have always been that way, but it wasn't until baseball proclaimed a Jackie Robinson Day that it really became part of the game's consciousness. Having everybody wearing his No. 42 is so cool.

People might not realize that while Dodgertown proper was fully integrated, Holman Stadium was not, per local ordinance. It wasn't until 1962 that—at the urging of players—separate-but-equal restrooms and drinking fountains were eliminated. So, even though Robinson had integrated the game, during his entire career, his home spring training stadium was segregated. Fittingly, Dodgertown is now called the Jackie Robinson Training Complex and is run by MLB.

I'm obviously not qualified to talk about what Robinson went through in Vero Beach. Newcombe occasionally would tell a story that would get the prejudicial point across. I know the Black players were not made to feel as comfortable as White players were at Vero Beach. That's a fact. I think we all benefitted by the fact that it was a really small town, pretty isolated, and that made it harder to get into trouble compared to teams like the Yankees who trained in Fort Lauderdale, where you had a lot of options. But it was still the Deep South and it wasn't a friendly environment for African American ballplayers.

I think it's a tribute to the Dodgers and to each international player that almost without exception they handled the challenging cultural adjustment professionally and without major drama. Of course, there are always exceptions, and the obvious one is Yasiel Puig. For pure talent, Puig was as gifted as any of them. When he first arrived, he was as much of a five-tool player as anybody I've seen come through the farm system. He could beat you in every phase of the game. And he was incredibly exciting, like Willie Mays exciting. But he played with reckless abandon off the field, too. He wasn't focused. He didn't take his job seriously. And he insisted on being the center of attention, which alienated his teammates. Fans and social media adored his antics, but it did him no favors. He ran himself out of the big leagues while he was still in his 20s.

Just like I can't imagine what Robinson went through, I'm sure going from living in poverty in communist Cuba to becoming an instant millionaire in the United States has its trappings for which most aren't ready. You need to have a good support group around you of people you can trust. Otherwise, people coming at you from different angles can lead you astray. Puig is the poster boy for how it can all go terribly wrong.

• CHAPTER 7 •

CLUBHOUSE POLICE

One of our greatest strengths in my years with the Los Angeles Dodgers was dealing with issues internally. It's just what we were about. We took care of our own problems. We policed ourselves before, during, and after the game. When something went awry—like a guy not running out a ground ball or not having a quality at-bat—those things were noticed. We didn't get into that person's face when that happened and make a scene, but there was a look. And usually that's all it would take to get the message across. One time it happened to me, and I knew it as soon as it happened. It was one of those meaningless at-bats that you have. You're up by eight runs in the bottom of the eighth inning and you lose a bit of focus. I think there was nobody on and one out, and we were well ahead, and I swung at a first pitch and hit a little ground ball to the second baseman. As soon as I started running to first base, I was thinking to myself, *What was that about?* I didn't have a purpose. It was just like, "Let's get the game over with. Let's go have fun in the clubhouse and move on to tomorrow." They would have had a better chance if somebody had been pinch-hitting because I was kind of just beyond where we were in the moment. And I came back to the dugout and I think Davey Lopes, Dusty Baker, and Bill Buckner gave me a look. I just kind of shook my head and said, "Yeah, it's on me, man. I got it." That's how we did it. We didn't let things go too far. We didn't let things fester.

For the most part, we got along pretty well, considering the friction that can develop when you spend as much time together as we did. But there seemed to be specific tension between Tommy Lasorda and Don Sutton. They never had a solid relationship. Sutton, who died of kidney cancer in 2021, considered himself The Man and he kind of demanded preferential treatment. For example, he wanted to park his Bentley, which he did, in a spot where nobody else did, where it's completely protected. The way he did it definitely rocked the boat. In spring training we flew to Tampa/St. Petersburg, Florida, for an overnight set against the St. Louis Cardinals and New York Mets, who shared a stadium. Sutton was supposed to pitch the first game. But he didn't make our plane out of Vero Beach. He just no-showed and didn't notify anybody. And if you've never been to Vero Beach, the airport is literally across the street from Dodgertown. You could walk there in five minutes. Back then, there was virtually no airport security. You just showed up and walked up the stairs onto the plane. It was impossible to miss a flight. But Sutton wasn't on the plane. So once airborne, Red Adams, our pitching coach, told Lasorda that Sutton wasn't on the plane. We landed, bussed to the field, got dressed for pregame workouts, and still no Sutton. Maybe a half hour before game time, Sutton showed up in the clubhouse. It turned out that he flew himself over. He had a pilot license and his own little plane and he decided to fly over and not give anybody a heads-up. Apparently, he didn't think a thing of it. He dressed and was just about to head out for warm-ups, and Adams had to tell him he's not pitching. And Sutton said, "Of course I'm pitching," and went off on a rant. And Lasorda came over, and they went into his office. And it wasn't like a screaming match, but Sutton came out of the meeting unhappy.

Sutton kind of pushed that envelope a little too much. He alienated some guys with stuff like that. He kind of operated on his own. We had a set of unwritten but universally applicable rules, and there weren't many, and then apparently there was a different set of rules that he operated under or tried to operate under. And sometimes it resulted in a confrontation. Lasorda and Sutton just didn't see eye to eye on much. Maybe it was because Sutton predated Lasorda. Sutton wanted to be the leader of the team, and a pitcher can't be the leader of the team. If you had Don Drysdale and Sandy Koufax standing up and saying something, that would work. I can see Clayton Kershaw being accorded the same respect, as much for the way he handles himself in the clubhouse as he does on the field. But your primary leadership has to come from the position guys who are playing every day; that's my opinion. Because they're playing five games to a pitcher's one (or four games to your one back in that time), they're just a bigger presence on how things go down every day.

Fortunately for us, we had a bunch of guys who had leadership qualities. We did things as a group. Lopes was named captain by Lasorda, but it was more a ceremonial title. If Lopes or I or anybody thought it was time to have a team meeting, anybody could speak up and call it. Usually, I would ask permission to have a players' meeting with no manager or coaches allowed, and everybody would speak their piece. We were able to air it out and we had almost a direct turnaround. Some managers are a little too insecure to be excluded from team meetings but not Walter Alston or Lasorda or some of the other notable managers like Tony La Russa, Joe Torre, Jim Leyland, Bruce Bochy, or Mike Scioscia. I think those guys were pretty secure in their positions to where they'd actually welcome the players taking it on.

Here's an example of how we handled issues before they spiraled out of control. Baker had a chance to tie a game with a hit with two outs in the ninth inning and instead he struck out, and the game ended in a loss. He came into the clubhouse, and I was walking over to my locker and he picked up one of those foldable chairs and threw it, and it hit me in the back. I knew he didn't mean to hit me, but it didn't feel good, and he didn't exactly apologize for it in the moment. No "I'm sorry, Penguin." No "I feel bad." He was more upset with how the game ended than he was that he hit me. And it just came off poorly, but we left it at that. And the first thing the next day, he came in and wanted to talk to me. And he said, "I went back to the hotel and I told Harriet [his wife] what happened after the game. And she said, 'Don't come back here tomorrow until you apologize.'"

Lasorda especially liked the fact that we would fix things ourselves; it made things easier for him. Having an infield like ours, getting to write the lineup every day when you have four pillars, isn't that a great thing? He didn't have to worry about who was playing second base that day. I think it was a huge asset. We were as united and as close as we could be under the circumstances. And we got things done. Our time was one of the best eras of Dodgers baseball. We held up our end of the bargain that was kind of laid before us, representing the organization as well as it had been in the past. That's what was handed down to us from Brooklyn, and I felt obligated that we needed to add to it. We had the longest running and most successful infield in MLB history. We had the first 30-home run foursome. On the '81 world championship team, every member of the team had been an All-Star at some point in time—with the exception of Steve Yeager. We had rookies of the year, Cy Young Award winners, and eventually we had World Series tri-MVPs. The facts are indisputable.

Maybe it was because of my relationship with Lasorda or my relationship with Peter O'Malley, but I usually was the one who asked Lasorda for permission to hold a team meeting without him. We'd go down to the old clubhouse, which was used by the Angels when they played at Dodger Stadium in the 1960s. Lasorda and the coaching staff were not invited. This was our meeting. That way guys would not be afraid to say what they needed to. We aired it out in the open, and it rarely was directed at anyone personally. It was more of an overall conversation. And if there was something that came up that you were directly involved in, that may have been addressed like, "Hey, I can't have you missing meetings anymore. I can't have you showing up late, can't have you missing the bus. This isn't good for us. We've got to work together as a team."

There were times over the course of a long season that we'd get a little lackadaisical. It's only normal. We just needed somebody to ring the bell. We didn't have a lot of rules on the road. Lasorda didn't set a curfew. We were grown men, we knew what our obligations were. If you wanted to go out and have a great time and mess up today or tomorrow or whatever, well, that wasn't going to last long. You would hear about it. Knowing that we'd police ourselves, Lasorda didn't have to. I think that was a good thing for us and for him.

Of course, for as long as we played together as a unit, there was bound to be the occasional dustup, and the one that rocked the boat the most was the 1975 Steve Garvey article written by Betty Cuniberti of *The (San Bernardino) Sun*. She quoted me and Lopes talking about Garvey, whose promotional personality had caused friction in the clubhouse. Even worse: her column included the most critical quotes—that none of Garvey's teammates liked him—attributed to an anonymous teammate. I'm not sure why she had to use anonymous quotes when she already had me and Lopes speaking on the record. It seemed she just wanted to stir things up. If that was the goal, it worked because it set off a firestorm, and Alston called a team meeting to remind everybody that we had a job to do, whether we liked each other or not. Airing dirty laundry in public was not the Dodgers' way. I'm not sure why, but it seemed like I was suspected of being the unattributed source and I was bearing the burden of these anonymous quotes. It's funny that I became a suspect, when I was one of the few willing to put my name on my quotes in the first place. Certain people seemed to just throw that on me, presuming the anonymous player was me. It wasn't. Pretty soon, O'Malley reached out and asked to have a closed-door meeting with me. He wanted my take on what was going on. I told him I was responsible for everything that's in that column that's behind my name. But I was not responsible for the anonymous quotes. I told him, "I know who they are. But that's not me." He said he believed me because of how adamant I was about it.

Every time we'd go to the east, there was an article saying the Dodgers were in chaos. I didn't feel like Garvey protected me there. I even apologized to him for what I did say. We talked one-on-one in the old Angels clubhouse under the field level and down the third-base line. I said, "I want to explain to you my position, what I said, because I am sorry if I personally brought any harm to you. I stand by what I said, but the other stuff, the anonymous stuff, that wasn't me and shouldn't be tied to me." Garvey seemed to accept what I said, and we moved on.

It was a trying time for the team, but personally I was getting crushed for things I didn't say. And I was left to make sure that I was not going to fall apart during the push to the end of that year. It should be noted that the controversy didn't tear our team apart. In fact, we went on to play another six years together, reaching the World Series three times and winning in 1981.

We had very few true scandals in my time with the Dodgers, but we weren't completely immune to them. Bob Welch battled alcoholism. Steve Howe was addicted to cocaine. But for the most part, we were pretty well-behaved. It wasn't until late in my career that I realized something was going on that was really changing the game. Dwight Evans asked me in 1987, when I was in my last year while playing for the Oakland A's, if I knew anything about teammates Mark McGwire and Jose Canseco on steroids. And I said, "I can't spell steroids. I really can't. All I can tell you is that these guys go into the weight room and press the building. They really do. They press the building."

Then I told him about a time when Canseco came in after batting practice. Above the left-field pavilion in Oakland was a seating area, then a brick walkway, then a little grassy place that's enclosed, and then the scoreboard. In other words, it's a long ways away. And Canseco came in after one batting practice and said, "Someday I'm going to hit it up in that green area. I'm going to hit the grass up there one of these days."

He was 23 years old, a cut specimen. He hit the ball as far as anybody. He and McGwire just obliterated batting practices. Their batting practices were audacious. They were hitting balls out of Chicago and Detroit, completely out of the yard. At that time four balls had been hit out of Dodger Stadium in history, and Willie Stargell had two of them. It was a feat. But things had begun to change. Playing on minor league fields in spring training, they'd have 50' high hitter's eye in center field 425' away, and these guys were launching bombs over these things. *Are you serious? Are you absolutely kidding me? What time did that flight leave?* Just amazing power. But I did not tune in to the why. Later on, you could see the physical differences. And players like McGwire physically broke down, which I think sometimes is a side effect. I think it was his feet that he had a problem with. Since that unfortunate day testifying in Congress, McGwire has pretty much fessed up and he is not hiding. And good for him. Canseco got blackballed from baseball, but the interesting thing with Canseco is that everybody that he mentioned was ultimately implicated. Well, it seems he wasn't lying.

I was sitting with George Brett behind home plate during a batting practice session at Dodger Stadium during the time of the McGwire–Sammy Sosa home run race. We just started laughing. You wonder if anything we did back then really meant anything. I mean, it was silly. They just buried balls all over the ballpark. My peer group was on the low level of meds—if you're talking about speed or greenies. It is my belief they are not performance-enhancing drugs. It's like they'd help me stay awake at night or give a little bit of energy, like strong coffee or an energy drink because you're dragging. It didn't reshape your body. I'm not going to tell you that I was a choirboy or a saint. I had my moments, but they were just a handful. It was in the heat of the summer, and we played a doubleheader, and I was dragging the next day. And I just wanted like a NoDoz you'd take to stay focused for studying. I didn't see that as an academic-enhancer and I didn't see it as a performance-enhancer. It was like a B-12 shot. Honestly, vitamin B-12 shots were more prevalent. You'd come back from an East Coast trip, the weather was rough, you'd have a cold or a cough, and you'd go into the training room, and our team doctor would give you a B-12 shot. But steroids are life-threatening. We saw that first with Lyle Alzado in the NFL and then, unfortunately, Ken Caminiti. What a horrible thing that must have been. I'm just glad that my group played and achieved our accomplishments before that ever became prominent in baseball.

As for the cocaine period, and specifically with the Dodgers' Howe, I was really unaware. Once the game started, the relievers would go down to the bullpen, and we didn't see those guys until after the game. Nobody looked sky high to me, but obviously Howe had a very serious problem. Before that Welch had detailed his alcoholism in his biography, *Five O'Clock Comes Early*. I didn't have to read the book. I realized it on a trip to San Francisco. Because of the weather at Candlestick Park, nobody went out to the ballpark early. Everybody took the late bus from the hotel. I was sitting on the bus before we left the hotel, and here came Welch, weaving down the bus aisle, slamming into the side of the seats, gabbing like crazy. I said to nobody in particular, "What's going on with him?"

He said, "I've been drinking all day, going from bar to bar."

His book details how hard it was for him to get off it. Lasorda was always very outspoken about addictions, saying it was a sign of weakness and a bad choice. I didn't think that was fair. Alcoholism is a disease.

I wasn't aware of anything with the Dodgers similar to Pete Rose's gambling on baseball, which got him banned from the game and prevented him from going into the Hall of Fame. It's a personal shame because there isn't anything in life he wanted more than to be a Hall of Famer. He talks about it all the time and he's obsessed with it, and it's been hard on him, but he made the mistake. He knew the rules.

This is the team photo of my 1960 Little League Giants before we played an exhibition game to entertain the detainees at the McNeil Island Corrections Center, which can be seen in the background. (Ron Cey)

My Washington State coach Chuck Brayton nicknamed me "Penguin" because of the I way waddled when I ran the bases, and it led to this clever Nike poster. (Nike)

I hang out with Rick Austin, who became my frat brother, best man, and lifelong friend, on the 1966–67 Cheney Studs. (Ron Cey)

Dodgertown in Vero Beach, Florida, had a great setup, including Holman Stadium and the heart-shaped lake, which was a valentine from Dodgers president Walter O'Malley to his wife, Kay. (O'Malley Seidler Partners, LLC)

We flew in style in the Dodgers-owned Boeing jet named "Kay O' II" in honor of Walter O'Malley's wife, Kay. Purchased in 1970, the airplaine was in use from the 1971 season through the 1982 season with Lew Carlisle at the helm. (O'Malley Seidler Partners, LLC)

I bat at Holman Stadium during an exhibition game with the Tokyo Yomiuri Giants in 1975. (O'Malley Seidler Partners, LLC)

I take a curtain call after hitting a grand slam against Steve Carlton and the Philadelphia Phillies in the 1977 NLCS. (AP Images)

I am in the batting cage at Holman Stadium in Dodgertown under the watchful eye of Dodgers manager Tommy Lasorda. (O'Malley Seidler Partners, LLC)

From left to right: commissioner Bowie Kuhn, Sparky Anderson, Tommy Lasorda, myself, and Davey Lopes hang out during spring training in March of 1979. (O'Malley Seidler Partners, LLC)

Showing how good an organization it was, the Los Angeles Dodgers threw Christmas parties for the kids at Dodgertown with fake snow, Santa Claus, and gift-wrapped presents for all. (O'Malley Seidler Partners, LLC)

Sandy Koufax, who throws batting practice to us, helped instill the strong culture within the Dodgers organization. (O'Malley Seidler Partners, LLC)

The tri-MVPs of the 1981 World Series: outfielder Pedro Guerrero, catcher Steve Yeager, and I celebrate defeating the New York Yankees. (AP Images)

Outside of Dodgers president Peter O'Malley's club-level office, he and Dodgers manager Tommy Lasorda proudly display the 1981 World Championship trophy. (O'Malley Seidler Partners, LLC)

From left to right, "The Infield" of myself, Bill Russell, Davey Lopes, and Steve Garvey is reunited at the 2013 Old-Timers' Game at Dodger Stadium. (AP Images)

I hang out with the great Hank Aaron. We not only played in the 1974 All-Star Game together, but I also was on the field when he hit his record-breaking 715th home run. (Ron Cey)

He may have played on the rival Giants, but Willie Mays was my idol. We hang out in 2018 during a 60th anniversary celebration honoring the Giants' and Dodgers' moves to the West Coast. (Ron Cey)

• CHAPTER 8 •

WHERE DO I RANK?

There are 268 players in the Hall of Fame; 17 of them were primarily known as third basemen, the lowest number for any position. For whatever reason, the hot corner just hasn't been a hotspot for elite recognition. I was not a Hall of Fame player. I was short of that. I'm not the 1 percent; I'm the 2 percent and I don't feel bad about that. I'm very proud to say that I finished my career with the highest total WAR of any player in the 1968 draft, not just the Los Angeles Dodgers. I did what I could. Though I honestly feel that in hindsight I should have done more, I'm not even sure how much more would have been good enough to get into the Hall of Fame. The prerequisites back then weren't broken down by position. It wasn't second basemen need to do this to get in, or shortstops need to do this, or third basemen need to do this. It was 3,000 hits and 500 home runs for a hitter and 300 wins for a starting pitcher. If you reached those benchmarks, you got in. And if you fell short and you had two players with relatively similar careers, but one had been on a winner or was constantly on a team like the Cincinnati Reds or the Dodgers or the New York Yankees, the chances of getting into the Hall of Fame were better than the other guy.

A few years ago when Tim Wallach was coaching for the Dodgers, the front office provided him a slew of analytical data to help him prepare for games. And Wallach was nice enough to let me know that had I played today's game with my performance from yesteryear, I would have been pretty proud of how that would be viewed by the analysts. Wallach is the first one who pointed out to me the work of people like Bill James, a historian and statistician generally credited for the sabermetric approach in understanding why teams win and lose, viewing the performance of players through a prism of new statistics such as runs created and range factor. James' work has been adopted by many front offices, including the Oakland A's, as described in the best seller and movie *Moneyball.* Stats such as WAR (wins above replacement) and WAA (wins above average) have evolved to further dissect a player's value.

James, in fact, once wrote that I was "substantially underrated." And when he compiled his "Best Players of the Last 50 Years" list a couple of years ago, he crunched the numbers at third base and was even more complimentary to me: "Mike Schmidt was unquestionably the dominant NL third baseman from the mid-70s to the late '80s, but Cey would have to be the No. 2. From 1973 to 1982, Cey was probably never any worse than the No. 4 NL third baseman in any given year, and about half that time he would probably be considered a solid No. 2 guy. In contrast to the family mentioned earlier (Wallach/DeCinces/Gaetti), Cey belongs to a different one. They share several of the same characteristics—.250 to .260ish average, 20 HRs a year, slow afoot, good defense—but with one key difference, the ability to take a walk, and therefore their OBPs tend to be higher, more in the .350 to .360 area. Cey is that type, and I would put him in a family with Sal Bando and Robin Ventura, players like that. Cey is probably never going into the Hall of Fame, but he was a very good, valuable, championship quality player. I have always been intrigued by the 1984 NL East champion Cubs, a team that ended a nearly 40-year postseason drought for that franchise. Cey was one of several veterans who had been assembled on that team who had prior World Series experience—Cey, Gary Matthews, Dave Lopes, Larry Bowa, Keith Moreland, Jay Johnstone, Richie Hebner,

Bob Dernier, Dick Ruthven. It was an intriguing blend of veterans who had been to (and even won) the World Series with other teams, along with younger up-and-coming stars like Ryne Sandberg, Leon Durham, and Jody Davis. It was fleeting, as they spent the next four seasons in fourth place or lower, and by the time they returned to the postseason in 1989, the team had pretty much been overhauled aside from Sandberg, Rick Sutcliffe, and Scott Sanderson, but it was a memorable season for the Cubbies."

Although metrics are relatively new to baseball, statistics have been a big part of the sport virtually since inception. We used comparable stats when I was the first Dodgers player to take the team—and beat it—in salary arbitration in 1975. I followed that with my best year. I had only one career high that season, but I had everything together. And when you apply today's analytics, it was my highest WAR. Even back then, the numbers convinced management I had a bright future, so they came to me with a three-year contract offer at a time when they didn't give three-year contracts. My agent and I were a little bit surprised by that, but free agency and arbitration were new to the scene, and the club wanted to get ahead of the curve and start locking players up long term to have cost certainty with their payrolls. The second year of that contract was 1977, when I had the greatest single offensive month in Dodgers history, and in early May, Peter O'Malley asked if I'd be interested in signing a five-year extension that would lock me in through 1983. How could I not accept that?

Nowadays, Juan Soto reportedly turns down $350 million because he knows he's going to be worth more. I can't imagine coming home to my wife, Fran, and saying, "Honey, I just turned down $350 million." Like, how much is enough? Do you really need to be the highest-paid player in the game? Or do you want to secure your family and just get this done and not worry about whether you're going to get an extra $10 million? I took the five years, and quickly after that, they extended Davey Lopes, Steve Garvey, and

Bill Russell. They locked up the whole infield, which was a big reason we stayed together as long as we did. That financial security, of course, meant no upward mobility for some talented Dodgers minor leaguers. From that point on, every door was shut to every minor league infielder. I'm sure we broke a lot of hearts. They were all playing in the minor leagues hoping to get traded, while we played every day in the major leagues. We didn't want to leave the door open. Everybody's heard the Lou Gehrig/Wally Pipp story. None of us wanted to be that guy. Garvey set the National League record for consecutive games played, but none of us wanted a day off. Our day off usually was flying cross country at the start or end of a road trip.

I got pretty sick going down the stretch of 1974 and still kept playing. I caught a little bit of a bug and was given the antibiotic tetracycline, which I'm still allergic to. It gave me an ulcerated tongue and I couldn't eat solid foods. I lost my strength, my performance nosedived, and I was really, really disappointed because I was prepared to finish strong. It wasn't indicative of how I should have finished, but you play 162 games for the first year or two, and it's a real grind. You have peaks and valleys and you have to be really well-equipped physically and mentally to get through those periods. And I learned from it. I fell a little bit short but eventually turned that around and got to where I felt like I was going to be able to hit 25 home runs and drive in 90 runs a year and play well defensively, and our teams were going to be right there in the mix every year.

That 1974 season was my first as an All-Star, and the National League won the game 7–2 in Pittsburgh. The Dodgers had four starters in the lineup—Jimmy Wynn, Garvey, Andy Messersmith, and me. Wynn, Garvey, and I had hits. I drove in two runs, and Reggie Smith came off the bench with a home run. It was a big Dodgers night and a big deal for me. I started at third base ahead of Schmidt. We were a few outs from winning this game, and Pete Rose, Johnny Bench, Joe Morgan, Henry

Aaron, and myself were in a small lounge area, and everybody was having a good time. Aaron asked, "Who's going to be the MVP of the game?"

Rose said, "Well, he's sitting right next to you," and everybody looked at me.

And Aaron said, "Oh, yeah, congratulations. It's getting late. You better get your jersey top on and get back out there because they're gonna want to interview you right after the game." Aaron played in 25 All-Star Games, and Rose played in 17, so they had to know what they were talking about. I knew I had a shot because I had that kind of a game, but the reality was kind of setting in. They convinced me. So, I headed back to my locker and put my stuff back on, and then the next thing I know, I was looking at the TV, and they announced that Garvey was the game MVP. Garvey had a pair of hits and played all nine innings because Tony Perez, who would have replaced him, was sick. The guys in the clubhouse looked at me kind of puzzled. I'll admit I was disappointed; it's only human nature. That kind of honor can change a guy's career.

On the other hand, spending those moments with legendary players, who thought I had the best game, was so cool. I was still in the early part of my career and I was in the same clubhouse and playing on their level in a show-case game. That was a big deal. I had sort of made it, climbing the ladder to a new plateau, and once you get there, you want to stay there. It's the same with winning the pennant. There isn't any place other than first place; it's what you're striving for. Second place will never be good enough after that.

My biggest team disappointment was losing the 1978 World Series. That should have been ours, and it wasn't. Athletes have a tendency to believe that their team was the best team—win or lose. The recent Dodgers team, which won the World Series in the year of COVID-19, probably believes it's the greatest team the Dodgers have ever put together.

The media adds to the narrative by echoing that. I know it's to get attention. I know it sells tickets. There's a reason behind it. But I'll take the other side of that. No knock on that Dodgers team, which is elite, but we turned Los Angeles into a Dodgers town. We went to four World Series in eight years. We had the record-breaking infield and the first foursome of 30-homer hitters. They're not us and they're not ever going to be us. You can't duplicate what we did.

We're proud of what we accomplished. Maybe even a little surprised. If you had told me prior to my career that I was going to do the things that I did, I probably would have said, "I'll take it." After the fact, I feel like I should have done a little bit more, but that's my nature. I wanted to drive in 100 runs every year and I fell short. A good example was my rookie year of 1973. I had a real shot at being Rookie of the Year the way I played in the first half, but I forgot to play the second half of the season. At the break I had nine home runs and 54 RBIs and I was hitting .266, and that projects to 20 homers and 100 RBIs, which I thought I would be able to achieve. Unintentionally, I really shut down after the first half, and it was a learning experience. I finished with a .245 average, 15 home runs, and 80 RBIs. The 80 RBIs were a Dodgers club record for a rookie. I made the All-Rookie team, was sixth for Rookie of the Year and ahead of Schmidt, who was a rookie the same season and went on to the Hall of Fame. But I just didn't finish it off.

In spring training the next year, I ran into Perez, who had played winter ball with me in Santurce, Puerto Rico, before my rookie season. And one of the first things that he said to me was, "Excuse me. You've got to play both halves." It's almost like he read my mind. He said, "You'll learn. It's a long season." When you get into your rookie year, there's a lot of things that you're really not aware of, and you kind of have to take these things as you go along. It was a learning experience for me.

Schmidt went on to be the greatest third baseman in baseball history statistically. He won home run titles. He was the league MVP three times. He won Gold Gloves, Silver Sluggers, made 12 All-Star teams. He was the whole package. I had some better seasons than he, but he had a better career. I am in that upper tier, but I also know that Schmidt ended up having a Hall of Fame career. George Brett did, too. From that point on, you can make your choices. Eddie Mathews is a Hall of Famer, Brooks Robinson is a Hall of Famer. Wade Boggs is probably in that group. Adrian Beltre should get there, and if there is one current third baseman headed to the Hall of Fame, it's Nolan Arenado if he stays healthy. He's a highlight film. In my opinion, he's the greatest defensive third baseman, and I don't care how many Gold Gloves Robinson won. If Robinson won 16 Gold Gloves, I should have one or two and I didn't. Gold Glove was a popularity contest like the All-Star Game. The Gold Glove process has become much fairer in recent years because they're allowing metrics to determine the finalists.

In his first year of eligibility, Ted Simmons received less than five percent of the writers' Hall of Fame votes and fell off the ballot. But 30 years after Simmons retired and through a newly popularized prism of analytics, the Modern Baseball Era Committee reconsidered and voted him into the Hall of Fame. I'm not saying that could or should happen to me, but analytics shed a different light on my career as well.

Like Simmons, I fell off the writers' ballot after one year. My teammate across the diamond, first baseman Steve Garvey, never received fewer than 20 percent of the writers' Hall of Fame votes and peaked at 42.6 percent. But I had a much higher career WAR than our first baseman (53.8 to 38.0), more home runs (316 to 272), and a higher OPS (.799 to .775). Metrics put me at the top of Dodgers position players offensively and defensively for a decade and right behind Mike Schmidt for National League third basemen. I led the Dodgers in offensive WAR six times and defensive WAR four times. Garvey never led the club in either category. My career WAR is higher than Brooklyn Dodgers first baseman Gil Hodges' 43.9, which is higher than Garvey's 38. The Golden Era Committee corrected another glaring oversight in 2022 by putting Hodges into the Hall of Fame.

You never heard the word *metrics* when I played. Our offense was described with words like *loaded*. Tommy Lasorda had his reasons for lining us up the way he did, but if we had come along in this generation, our batting order would have looked different. Even without sophisticated data, I always thought I should have been hitting ahead of Garvey. I think today's metrics, and the way they are incorporated into lineup construction, would bear that out. Until Wallach alerted me to the new-school theories, it was just my gut. Nobody really tried to educate me with it or asked me if I wanted to know about it. But Wallach said, "You're not going to believe some of this stuff."

And then I started to pay attention and did some research on it. And it made me think, *Why didn't I know this when I was playing?* When someone asked my favorite player, Willie Mays, why he was the only player to hit 30 home runs and steal 30 bases four times in a career, his response was: "If I had known it was so important back then, I'd have done it more times." That's kind of how you have to look at the way the game changes.

But I felt back then and I feel today that it makes more sense to have a power hitter, who walks a lot, batting fourth as opposed to another guy, who doesn't, because one guy is going to create more situations, and the other guy is going to end more situations. I would have been moving guys up on base for Garvey to drive them in. Garvey had a lot of tools in his batting toolbox, but walks weren't one of them. He liked to swing the bat. I was more disciplined with the strike zone and was happy to take a walk if that's what the pitcher gave me. From 1977 to 1981, I had more at-bats in the fifth spot than I did anyplace else. The lineup rarely varied from this starting eight—Lopes, Billy Buckner, Smith, Garvey, myself, Baker, Rick Monday, Steve Yeager. In 1981 Pedro Guerrero got in there because Smith was hurt. But Guerrero was still hitting lower then; he moved up in the order when most of us left. I felt that the best overall player who could fit all the parameters of a third hitter was Smith. He could hit for power, he was going to drive in runs, he could hit from both sides of the plate, and he would steal some bases once in awhile. Plus, he'd walk. There wasn't any other guy we had who could do all of that as well as Smith, and it's a tough spot.

Now they don't construct lineups the same way. You now see power guys leading off or hitting second because they want these guys to have that extra at-bat, so they push them all up. The Chicago Cubs moved Anthony Rizzo up there when he was slumping, and he caught fire. The Yankees moved up Aaron Judge and sometimes they put Giancarlo Stanton higher. The Dodgers lead off with Mookie Betts. Now with the universal designated hitter, the National League can maneuver in ways it couldn't before because teams can put a guy with speed down there at the end like the American League used to do. They're going to score more often. With the old-time lineups, you could be in a hole there. You could have three light hitters at the bottom of the order and you're not scoring runs down there. They don't play that game anymore because you have guys who are going to hit the ball out of the park batting seventh and eighth. They don't steal bases much because they don't want to get those guys thrown out.

A lot of these lineup decisions or "suggestions" are actually made by the front office with data generated by a team of statistical analysts, not by an autocratic manager like in my day. That's one way technology has advanced the game. Another way is in the clubhouse. I've seen how they break down films today compared to what little we did, and the technology is quite amazing. They use virtual reality headsets, allowing hitters to visualize an opposing pitcher's delivery and the flightpath of the pitch. It's all so high-tech now. But if we didn't have much information then, there's so much data now that I think current ballplayers can kind of suffer paralysis by analysis. Not every player has the necessary aptitude to instantly process that much information. Some can; some can't. When you're out on the field, you have to have a clear mind. If you start crunching too much data, it's just so easy to be thinking, *It's a 3–2 count, and 75 percent of the time he throws a certain pitch in this situation.* You become more of a guess hitter rather than being able to make an adjustment to a different pitch. You're looking fastball away and you get a breaking ball, and it's right there, and you freeze and take it. You should be making an instantaneous adjustment to hit the breaking ball, especially with men on base, and not be so programmed that you get stunned by a surprise. When you get a hanging slider, you've got to jump all over it. Just because it's a slider and you were looking fastball shouldn't prevent you from being a hitter, but it seems like it happens a lot that way. It's hard to be successful guessing both pitch and location on a regular basis.

Too many players from my generation are resistant to new-school methods, and when I see shifts that put the third baseman in right field or use four outfielders, I don't blame them. I'm in a more reflective time in my life, looking at things a little bit differently. I'm aging, hopefully growing as a person, starting to understand better. You start to be less critical. For obvious reasons, I'm a proponent of the WAR statistic. I'm the No. 1 Los Angeles Dodgers infielder of all time in WAR, and that means a lot to me. From the time I first started playing ball, I always had something rolling around the back of my head that a walk was as good as a hit. Go back far enough in Major League Baseball, and walks were counted as hits, and then they changed the scoring rules. Either way, it raises the on-base percentage, which I always felt was more important than average.

Ron Cey As Dodgers Stats Leader (By Year And Category)

1974	1975	1976	1977	1978	1979	1980	1981
GWRBI	HR	HR	GWRBI	WAR	HR	R	HR
	RBI	RBI			SF	BB	BB
	IBB	IBB			WAR	WAR	OPS
	SF	BB				GWRBI	OPS+
	OPS	OPS					WAR
	OPS+	OPS+					HBP
	WAR	WAR					
	GWRBI	GWRBI					

Dodgers All-Time WAR Ranking (Position Players)

1. Pee Wee Reese (68.4)
2. Duke Snider (65.3)
3. Jackie Robinson (61.7)
4. Zack Wheat (60.0)
5. Willie Davis (54.6)
6. Ron Cey (47.7)

On the other hand, I still have trouble when I see a manager rigidly stick to pitch counts, especially if it means yanking a pitcher working on a no-hitter or perfect game. If you showed me that these pitch counts really prevent pitching injuries, I could be persuaded. But pitchers are blowing out faster than ever. So that's a bogus excuse.

I also have trouble watching hitters persistently pull into the teeth of a shifted defense when a little bat control to send pitches the opposite way would be a simpler and easier way to success. You see the occasional exception, like when the Dodgers shifted against the Atlanta Braves' Ozzie

Albies in the 2021 playoffs. He had two strikes, and they were pitching to the outer half of the plate. That's real cocky. That's assuming the hitter is stubborn and won't punch a pitch the other way. Albies just stuck his bat out and hit a little roller down the third-base line, and there was nobody there. If guys can just handle the bat like that, it's a hit, but they don't teach that and don't reward it.

Then there are the bullpen games necessitated in part by a shortage of legitimate starting pitchers. The manager has an opener and a handful of guys lined up to follow. I hate bullpen games because they're just glorified exhibition games. They line up these relievers to face a certain stretch in the opposing batting order. Then the opponent can pinch hit to try to defeat this inning-by-inning relief strategy. I can't help it, but I'm from an era where it was "let's just go play." Similarly, they have scheduled days off now for position players. Our scheduled day off was literally a travel day when there wasn't a game scheduled. Sometimes you look at the lineup and wonder, *Did they call up the Double A team? These guys all need a rest at the same time?*

Then there are the shifts. This is a baseball purist's nightmare. They used to move everybody over as a group. Now, they singularly move one guy—like a third baseman to short right field—and then the rest stay in their positions. And so now you have a third baseman making a catch that's down the right-field line in foul territory, like a Manny Machado, and it's a pop-up to third base? Wait a minute, that's got to be wrong in the box score. I'm still lost with the shift because even if you instruct every pitcher the best way to pitch a certain hitter, every pitcher is different, and no hitter hits different pitchers the same way. That's when I really got lost.

The Dodgers lost a playoff game in 2015 because of the shift. When shortstop Corey Seager was a rookie, he forgot to cover third base, allowing Daniel Murphy to go from first to third on a walk. For a moment Seager didn't realize that with the third baseman shifted to right field for a left-handed pull hitter, it was his job to cover third base. It was heads-up base running by Murphy. Don't pick on Seager. We all have stories to tell about embarrassing moments in our early years, including me.

I was facing Bob Gibson, and it was my first time up against him. He shut us out on three hits, and I got one of them. But during my second at-bat, he struck me out on three pitches, and all of them were his pitches. The last one was a pitch he threw in on me, and I tried to get to it and then I tried to hold up, but I lost partial control of the bat, and it slid around my waist like a hula-hoop before it fell to the ground. I stood there for a moment all tied up. I really didn't know what even happened. *Was it a strike? Did I swing? Am I out? All of the above?* I finally picked up the bat and walked back to the dugout with my head down. I got to the dugout, started walking down the steps into the dugout, and saw probably 10 guys looking at me from the floor kind of laughing with me or at me. What else can you do? I'm glad it was Gibson, a future Hall of Famer, rather than somebody else. That's always been the story that I've told for years and years about my most embarrassing moment.

CHAPTER 9

MY HEROES

Remember collecting baseball cards, stacking originals in numerical order, and clipping the duplicates into bike spokes so it sounded like a motorcycle? That was me. My hero worship of sports stars is just as strong now as that simpler time as a kid in Tacoma, Washington. In that way I never grew up and I make no apologies. I display several dozen baseballs in my home office, and each was signed by a Hall of Famer. Despite 15 major league seasons, I never grew jaded or took for granted how fortunate I've been to meet, know, and even play against some of my childhood heroes. And I always remember that those players paved the way for the rest of us to chase our dreams. I'm grateful to every one of them.

Dodgers fans, please forgive me, but at the top of my heroes list is a Giants player. I can't really pinpoint how a kid from Washington state became obsessed with an Alabaman who began his professional journey in the Negro Leagues, made his Major League Baseball debut with the New York Giants in 1951, and continued his legendary career in San Francisco, where he remains a treasured icon. But for me, Willie Mays was Mike Trout, Ken Griffey Jr., and Barry Bonds all rolled into one. If you never saw him play, do yourself a favor and go to YouTube right now and prepare to be amazed. To me, he was Willie Amazing.

Growing up in the 1950s, we obviously didn't have YouTube, the Internet, or ESPN. We could watch a Major League Baseball game on television once a week. We had five local channels on TV. *Five*. No cable, no satellite, no streaming. We had radio basically. The first television game I ever saw was a Brooklyn game from Ebbets Field. I only remember one scene of it—this one image of the left-field pavilion and signboard outfield fences. But somehow we accumulated a lot of information. My love grew for the game, and I became a student of it. We knew player stats from the back of their Topps cards. We kept up with their daily results through the box scores in the newspaper.

Although Major League Baseball didn't arrive in my home state until 1969, we had a Triple A team in Tacoma, and it brought Mays to life for me in the form of an exhibition game I attended when I was 12. From that point on, Mays wasn't a guy who was playing in San Francisco. I saw him in my town, and he became real. I mean, I got to see my guy up close and personal.

And even in my formative mind, seeing Mays in person was a big step in nurturing my career goal of playing Major League Baseball. Before that, the professional athlete who made the biggest impression on me was Elgin Baylor, who helped lead Seattle University to the Final Four before going on to a Hall of Fame career with the Los Angeles Lakers. He was the first local sports star, and I remember thinking, *If he can do that, maybe I can do something like that.* He gave me a feeling that I had a chance, that local kids were performing really well, and that they're getting national attention. It demonstrated that people from this part of the country could be elite athletes. And it was kind of an early hope. I went on to play baseball, but in my youth, I played enough basketball to appreciate Baylor.

Mays, though, was the role model I idolized. Baseball was my first love. Basketball was over there, but baseball came first. One of my vivid memories about Mays, oddly, came when I went with my dad to a place called Sea-Tac Speedway, where my dad would race stock cars on the weekend on an old asphalt track. My dad would race in several heats, and there would be some down time between heats. I'd watch him race, and then during the down time, a bunch of us kids would run off to a play area, and I'd always bring a ball and glove and bat. And on that Sunday, I knew the Giants were playing, and we had a radio that could get the Giants broadcasts from San Francisco. That was the day Mays hit four home runs. And I was running around screaming, "Willie Mays hit four home runs. Willie Mays hit four home runs."

I wanted to hit home runs like he did. All my friends used to love Mickey Mantle, and I did, too. It was hard not to. It's funny, but back then I didn't think it was cool to admit you had idols and I kind of hid it for awhile. But I finally realized that was kind of ridiculous. You're only putting on this act or lying to yourself. What's the big deal about being able to just stand up and say, "Willie Mays, he's my man?" And I did, and it felt really good. And from that point on, I was good with it. But I kind of chastise myself a little bit, shoving it in the background for so long.

I sort of made up for it in 2018. During a series between the two rivals in San Francisco, the Giants held a 60-year anniversary of the moves to the West Coast by the Giants and the Dodgers and they invited me along with a few other Dodgers to participate. Meanwhile, I'd had a picture from the late 1970s of me by the batting cage and Mays, who was then traveling with the Giants as a coach. That photo was a real keeper, the first time I remember telling him he was my favorite player, and this anniversary event was going to be my best (and maybe my last) chance to get that photo signed.

I contacted the Giants front office about my desire for a meeting with Mays. One of the Candlestick Park clubhouse guys I knew from my playing days was still working in the new ballpark. So, I walked over to the Giants' side with the clubbie and got kind of excited, carrying this photo I'd had for quite some time. Mays looked really good in that picture, too, like he could still play. I got over there, and Mays couldn't have been more gracious. We spent about 20 minutes together—me and my idol. Who gets to do that in their life?

Mays was having a little bit of trouble signing, which was understandable at his age, but I reminded him one more time that he had been my favorite player since I was seven or eight years old. That made him smile, and it made me feel good to tell him. I gave him a hug, said good-bye, and it was just great. It was so cool for me to be able to see him play as a kid, to have an opportunity to play against him, to tell him what he meant to me. Thinking about that day still gives me goose bumps. And while Mays was always my No. 1 guy, the impact sports heroes had on me was overwhelming. I've got a collection of baseballs signed by Henry Aaron, Ted Williams, Joe DiMaggio, Stan Musial, Carl Yastrzemski, Rickey Henderson, Tom Seaver, and it goes on and on. It's just silly, super legendary guys. I had a chance to experience all of that. It's really just wild.

Despite signing so many autographs myself during and after my playing days, I was a little sheepish about asking for one—at least until after I retired. When I played, I never thought about starting a collection of signed baseballs. Once my playing career was over, I sort of jumped into it. I know that's kind of backward, wanting autographs in retirement after bypassing the chance when it would have been easy. Talk about missing the boat. But going to Old Timers' Games, seeing my peers, and not knowing when I'd see them again planted the memorabilia seed in me. No longer having daily access, I started getting addresses and contact information of legendary players. It started with Phil Niekro. I sent him a letter, and he sent back one of those postcards saying he was glad he could do it for me. And he mentioned that I was really tough on him as a hitter. I did the same thing with Rod Carew, who also wrote something back and with Yastrzemski and a number of other guys. It's nice to have this relationship because we are that kind of a fraternity. It does mean a lot to us.

We played an exhibition game against the California Angels when I was with the Chicago Cubs in Mesa, Arizona. It was pregame, we had just finished up with our batting practice, and they were about to take theirs. Our kids were there, and my son, Daniel, walked over to Reggie Jackson in the Angels dugout with a bunch of baseball cards, and he asked Jackson to sign them, and Jackson wasn't in the mood. He said no. That's just Jackson being Jackson, but Daniel came back to our side pretty disappointed and told me what happened. I said, "Well, let's go over there."

And I said to Jackson, "I want to introduce my son to see if you could sign a couple of baseball cards."

And he said to Daniel, "Weren't you just over here? Why didn't you tell me you're family?" He signed everything Daniel wanted.

Being from Washington state, the first local sports star I remember was Baylor. We didn't meet until we both were in Los Angeles, where he was the longtime general manager of the Los Angeles Clippers after his playing career with the Lakers. We became friends, attending each other's charity events, and that gave me the chance to tell him that I remembered how he put Seattle University basketball on the map. I was young, but I saw a few of their games. I saw him score 60 points. He had a flair about him. He was known for his body control, his hang time. It seemed like he'd go up, and one defender would go by, and another defender would try to swat at the ball, and a last guy tried, and he was still able to get off a perfect shot. It was amazing. And he was only about 6'5".

Seattle/Tacoma wasn't exactly a factory for superstar athletes. Most of my heroes were based far away, including Aaron, Wilt Chamberlain, Oscar Robertson, Kareem-Abdul Jabbar, Jesse Owens, of course Jackie Robinson, even Muhammad Ali. Eventually, though, I got to meet most of them as they came through Southern California.

I played against Aaron and with him as an All-Star. In 1974 the Atlanta Braves came to L.A. not long after Aaron broke Babe Ruth's all-time record of 714 home runs, which he did the first week of the season against us in Atlanta. I had two posters and two baseballs that I wanted to have him sign. I didn't know exactly how I was going to do that, so I just decided to take the bull by the horns and I walked across the field into the Braves dugout and up into the clubhouse. (Walking into an opposing clubhouse is not common practice.) Aaron wasn't at his locker, but when he got there, he saw me and smiled. I said, "I'm not going anywhere until these balls and posters are signed."

He said, "No problem," and was great about it.

When Aaron homered off Al Downing to set the new record, that was an epic moment in my career, just being part of a truly historic event. I remember watching the swing, seeing left fielder Bill Buckner climbing the fence in a desperate attempt to delay the inevitable, even though he really had no chance to catch it. As Aaron got to second base, Davey Lopes and Billy Russell had a brief chance to shake his hand. A few strides later, two kids ran onto the field, trying to share Aaron's spotlight, running alongside and slapping him on the back. Aaron gently tried to push them away. At this point, I was kind of debating what I would do when Aaron reached me because I really did want to shake his hand, too. But I also felt like it was his moment and I shouldn't interrupt it.

I didn't mind that the other guys did it because it was second base and a little farther from home plate. I was thinking, *What should I do?* And once these kids didn't back off and I didn't have a clear shot at him, I thought it might be even more distracting if I tried. At that point, it was best just to let him get to the plate. So I just let him go. Our catcher, Joe Ferguson, walked up the third-base line just to get out of the way of what was happening at home plate and shook his hand.

You're never supposed to root for an opponent, but I had to make an exception this time. There are occasions when the sport becomes even bigger than any one game. Candidly, I was thrilled to be part of this moment. I wanted this to happen, I really did. I suppose it's like those guys who played in the game when Cal Ripken Jr. broke the record for consecutive games played. Aaron came into the season needing one homer to tie Babe Ruth and two for the record. The Braves were in Cincinnati for Opening Day, and he homered for the tie. I figured he'd break the record in Cincinnati, but Aaron said he was hoping to do it at home, and we were scheduled for that first series in Atlanta. He sat out Atlanta's second game in Cincinnati but returned to the lineup for the series finale with the Reds and went 0-for-3. The next three games for the Braves were against the Los Angeles Dodgers. After Aaron's home run off Downing, they shut down the game for about a half-hour ceremony. It was really unforgettable, even though we lost the game 7–4.

A close second on my memory meter was playing against Mays in New York in 1973. He was finishing out his career with the Mets and wasn't the player of his prime, but he was still Willie Mays to me. He hit a home run against us, and as he came toward me at third base, I put my glove up to my face to hide a smile. *Are you kidding me? My idol just hit a home run, and he's going to go right past me?* I wanted to shake his hand, but I didn't. These days, opposing players walk up to the plate and just about give each other a hug. In my time, you'd get fined by the league for fraternizing. Times change, and I get it now. I love telling the stories of Mays' and Aaron's home runs because I was part of it. I know some people feel badly for Downing because, even though he was a really good pitcher and remains today a true gentleman and cherished friend, he'll always be remembered as the guy that gave up No. 715.

I was never compared to Mays for obvious reasons, but as my game developed as a youth, I starting hearing comparisons to another future Hall of Famer, Chicago Cubs third baseman Ron Santo. The comparisons began when I was 16 and were easy to make. Santo was also from the Seattle area, was also a third baseman, and even had the same first name. That's the first time I remember hearing that I was going to be the next Ron Santo. I didn't know what to do with it. I was 16 years old, and that's nice, but I was a kid, and he's a baseball star. At this point he was already a really good player. But because he was from just up the street in Seattle, it helped me solidify in my mind that maybe I could be that guy, too. Being compared to Santo actually made me think that there might be a possibility. It was hope, and that's what kind of made me work as hard as I did. When I went out and played baseball in the rain and mud while my family wanted to go to the lake or something, it was really simple. That sacrifice is what it was going to take.

The comparisons to Santo are flattering. Our career yearly offensive average stats are very similar across the board, though his WAR was higher. Defensively, I outranked him, but he won five Gold Gloves while I was overshadowed by Mike Schmidt. We both won the Lou Gehrig Award. He had me in All-Star Game appearances 9–6, but his Cubs were blanked reaching the postseason, while my club won five division titles and a World Series. We were both Washington natives, our birthdays were only 10 days apart, and we even wore the same uniform number.

Roberto Clemente was another player who impacted me even before he died a hero when the plane he chartered to provide earthquake relief in Nicaragua crashed while taking off from Puerto Rico. He had just reached the 3,000-hit mark in the major leagues, and I was in Puerto Rico to play Winter Ball for Frank Robinson when that tragedy happened. Clemente would have been the most exciting player of his day if there hadn't been a Mays. That's how dynamic Clemente was. I figured I would run into him playing in Puerto Rico. We were staying in a San Juan Hotel near the harbor—not far from where his plane crashed. It was around 2:00 in the morning, and some other players and I had just returned from a night out. We got to the room and turned on the TV. The sound was down, but you could tell something bad had happened, and the news bulletin caught my eye. I couldn't believe it. What a great player and great person who gave his life trying to help those in need!

A lot of my heroes weren't baseball players. Chamberlain and I used to work out at the same athletic club, the Mid-Valley Club, and we'd often play racquetball. He was an amazing athlete, utilizing his height to dominate volleyball games. With that wingspan he could cover the entire racquetball court without moving, and you couldn't get a ceiling ball past him. He was always in the way. We'd call hinders or interference, and being the competitor he was, he'd get pissed off. He told me he was probably a better bowler than basketball player. We got along great and would run into each other at various events around town. I've got a picture with him and Christine McVie of Fleetwood Mac taken at a fund-raiser at the Playboy mansion. We were like Mutt and Jeff. He was 7'1", and I'm 5'10". We were a ridiculous-looking pair. He also had this crazy idea of me and him competing in a pentathlon of five events each. He was serious. So I said, "Let's have a draft of events. You go first." I expected him to pick bowling based on the way he bragged about his bowling. He didn't let me down, but I was ready to fire back. "Okay, I take free-throw shooting." If you ever saw Chamberlain try a free throw, you'll know why.

His response was priceless: "Fuck you, Penguin. This pentathlon is officially over." And with a big smile, he shook his finger and said, "You got me." Technically, I guess, I won the the pentathlon by forfeit.

I've got a photo with Abdul-Jabbar where he's sitting and I'm standing, and our heads are the same height. Abdul-Jabbar has always been a huge Dodgers fan. He's probably the most thoughtful, articulate athlete I've ever known. I had followed his career ever since hearing about him as a high school star in New York, where he was All-Everything. You knew he was destined for greatness. Somehow John Wooden and UCLA got him out here, and they won NCAA championships every year. He went to the Milwaukee Bucks in the NBA, then landed with the Lakers. I remember meeting him for the first time. I was still playing for the Dodgers. While walking down the hallway outside the clubhouse, I saw him coming. I introduced myself and he said, "I'm hip. I know who you are."

From that point on, we'd always talk when we saw each other. He's always been a joy to be around. I have total respect for him and the way he's handled his life. He's on the right side of things, and I have tremendous admiration for him.

Ali actually was a figure who came on a lot later for me, but I admired him for what he stood for. Being defiant back then against the Vietnam War was really difficult for a lot of people to understand. But it turned out to be a war that was unnecessary. And it was the one that I nearly had to participate in. My wife, Fran, took part in peaceful demonstrations to bring awareness to the issue, and that was the time of the Kent State killings and the trial of the Chicago Seven. It was a very volatile time.

And the way Ali stood up for his beliefs really made an impact on me. He used his platform to make the world a better place. He energized the sport of boxing and he crossed over into other communities because he was funny, smart, fearless, and an excellent promoter. He was smarter than the rest of us. For example, there's technically no reason why he should have won the George Foreman fight at that point in time, but he found a way to maneuver and strategize to make it happen. He was just one of those guys who understood how to get it done, and that's something I really admire.

Our paths finally crossed in Las Vegas. After the 1977 World Series, Frank Sinatra invited Tommy Lasorda and me and our wives to Las Vegas to be a part of his program for the weekend. He was doing two nights at Caesars Palace and he was going to take care of the whole weekend. He took us to a restaurant in the hotel, where he had a room set aside and took care of everything. The next night we were going to the show. We were in the lobby with a group of people, and there's Ali. And Fran, who was even more starstruck than I, said she had to get Ali's autograph. He was very kind and took a picture with her and he signed whatever she had and spoke with her. I was a kid in a candy store. What a night: a cocktail party, the show, and dinner with Sinatra! I was so lucky. Who wouldn't want to trade places with me that night?

It didn't mean anything at the time to me, but as you might have noticed, most of my childhood heroes were African Americans. It didn't even occur to me back then; that's how color blind I was. I grew up around a fully integrated Boys Club and I wasn't taught to be prejudiced. We were just kids who played ball together. I just didn't hear ugly stereotyping. I only saw kids who wanted to play and wanted to win, just like me. We were just friends. I remember a kid named Charlie Williams from Stadium High School in Tacoma. He was a few years older than I, and he went to Seattle University after Baylor did. I went to one of his high school games when I was in junior high school, and Williams just went off, pouring in 38 points, and it was just great. I went nuts in this gym, and it's obviously something I never forgot. Williams eventually played pro ball in the old ABA for the Pittsburgh Pipers and teamed with Connie Hawkins to win the ABA title in 1968.

Not all of my heroes were superstars. Ron Billings and Don Moseid made huge impacts on my life and career. Oddly, both were basketball coaches—Billings at Stewart Junior High and Moseid at Mount Tahoma High School. They got the most out of me. They worked me, they pushed me, and they challenged me to a point where I wasn't only playing for myself; I was playing for them because they put in a lot of work with me. And this was diligent work. I mean, they were into it. They helped develop my character. They taught me winning, doing things right, understanding responsibilities, and responding to challenges. If you play team sports early on, you learn how to work with others while working toward a common goal. You learn reliability, responsibility, respect. It's all woven together. They were the coaches who I admired the most. It wasn't an old-school Bobby Knight thing, though at the time I actually felt like I could play for a guy like Knight (outside of the chair throwing and humiliation part of it). My coaches didn't do that. They didn't humiliate people. This was a relationship of learning, not by tearing you down. There was a plan that kept you interested and involved despite the hard work that was needed to hone your skills. So when practice was done, you went the extra mile. You shot another 25 free throws because you knew how important free throws were. Free throws are a gimme, and you have to capitalize on these. And the only way that you can take advantage of it is by practicing. And when it's crunch time, you're better prepared to take advantage of it.

It was work ethic. You hear about guys who are gym rats, they're in the gym all the time. Yeah, I get it. They turn on the lights in the morning and shut them off at night. I had a hoop in my backyard, and it might have been 35 or 40 degrees outside, but I was playing basketball. I needed to be dedicated. I didn't have the greatest physical body. I wasn't 6'2", 200 pounds, running the 100 meters in 10 seconds. I couldn't lift the building or jump out of the gym.

It's no surprise why I had so much admiration for Pete Rose. He was a switch-hitter, and every single day in batting practice, you would see him hitting from both sides of the plate. It didn't matter if the Reds were facing a right-handed pitcher or left-hander, Rose would take his swings from both sides of the plate every single day. It was his way of preparing and feeling comfortable. From my coaches at school to Walt Alston and Lasorda, I learned lessons that I carried with me the whole time. Each demanded a certain amount of excellence. They didn't put a lot of restrictions on you. We didn't really have curfew on the Dodgers. We were treated as adults. You understood that if you didn't perform, it's on you. This was your livelihood. You'd like to think that you would spend the time and care on all of that so that you can have a long career. But fitness wasn't as big a deal back then as it is today. I mean, I know guys who did very little in the offseason. I couldn't do that. If I went to spring training without having done the needed training and got hurt, I'd spend the whole time down there recovering from an injury suffered because I didn't prepare myself in the offseason.

Billings, my junior high school coach, handed me off to my high school coach, Moseid. Then Billings left the junior high school to coach at Lincoln High School in Tacoma. That was my mom's school and one of our rivals. That pitted me against my former teacher. And honestly, he was the one coach who had pretty good success against me because he knew me so well. He could defend me better. He knew the things that I did well and not so well, and so that was a challenge. I always wanted to beat Lincoln, but I also wanted to beat him. It was fun. I enjoyed that competitive level of it. There's a certain aspect of football and basketball that I played and learned that translated into baseball. I've had the good luck to grow up with so many heroes, but at this point in my life, my heroes are my family—my wife, my children, and the grandchildren they've given us. One more thing about heroes: it's an honor to be considered one, as I learned when Gregg Jefferies, a two-time All-Star, sought me out to tell me I was his favorite player growing up.

• CHAPTER 10 •

BILLY BUCK

Of all my teammates, Bill Buckner was my closest friend. I still can't believe he's gone. Buck died in 2019 of Lewy body dementia. He was 69. Buck was a fabulous athletic talent and a better person. He deserved better than to be defined by a ground ball through the legs. Baseball is cruel that way. You can have a 16-year, big league career, win a batting title, and be an All-Star but be known forever for an error. When I hear the phrase, "Life's not fair," I think of Buck.

I remember watching Game Six of the 1986 World Series, featuring Buck's Boston Red Sox vs. the New York Mets. Boston was one out away from winning its first World Series since 1918. Three straight singles and a wild pitch tied the game, and Mookie Wilson's soft grounder somehow rolled through Buckner's legs at first base for a walk-off win. It tied the series, the Mets won Game Seven, and Buckner became a Boston goat for life.

I felt so bad for Buck. You don't want this to happen to anybody. It's just a nightmare. The ball just didn't come up, and he didn't get his glove down there where it should have been. And you saw him walk off the field feeling as low as a ballplayer can feel. And if you remember that game and that inning, there were just so many different things that happened leading up to it. Crazy things, wild pitches, but all anybody really remembers is Buck and the ground ball. It was all on Billy Buckner.

I think, psychologically, I'm not gonna say it destroyed him. But the amount of abuse that he took was enough to crush anybody. And here was a friend of mine involved in this play that seemed to define his entire career. It's just so unfair in so many different ways. As a player, you have to accept the good and the bad. You talk about the good when it happens and you have to be able to talk about something bad when it comes up. You have to address it. You have to face that little demon. But it seemed that every time somebody had something to say about Buck, it was always related to that play. He sort of went into seclusion after that. I don't really remember seeing him at the ballpark or anywhere after that.

As MLB.com columnist Mike Lupica wrote after Buckner's death: "The punishment never fit the baseball crime with Buckner, who deserved better from everybody." Lupica's column recalled comedian Larry David's *Curb Your Enthusiasm* episode that made Buckner a hero. If you haven't seen the episode, Lupica described it: "There was a long and funny and *Curb*-like setup to the ending of that episode, one I believe is as famous as David has ever had in what has become an iconic series, one that involved Larry making a big error in a softball game and later meeting Buckner, who tells David not to worry, that people finally forgave him. Finally at the end, Larry and Buckner ended up outside a burning New York building. There is a mother in a window a few floors up with her baby and firemen down below with a jumping sheet as smoke continues to pour out of the building. Then the mother tosses the baby. The fireman's sheet is in a perfect position, and the baby lands on it. But because this is *Curb*, the baby bounces back up into the air, while we see all sorts of frantic reaction shots from the people in the crowd.

"And then Buckner, who's just told Larry that he just happened to be out for a walk from his hotel down the street, is running to catch the baby. At the last second, Buckner dives and lays out and ends up on his back, smiling, with the baby safely in his arms. At which point a New York crowd goes wild for Bill Buckner. 'Nice catch, Bill!' Larry yells.

"The next thing you see are members of the New York crowd putting Bill Buckner up on their shoulders. If you are a *Curb* fan, as I am, you know there really are so many memorable episodes in the series. But there was never a better or funnier or more memorable one than Bill Buckner's in Season Eight. I asked David about the episode, and about Buckner, after we all learned of Buckner's passing on Monday, a sad occasion whose only saving grace turned out to be this: Bill Buckner's death also became an occasion for people to remember what a truly great hitter he was in the big leagues. 'Very sweet, kind man,' David said. 'There was something about him that made me feel for the guy. What an awful thing to go through.'

"David said the idea for the show was submitted by a writer in Chicago, Pat McNelly, and at first they had all kicked around the idea of Buckner dropping the baby. But no one wanted to do that to Buckner. 'I saw that show in editing for weeks,' David said. 'And every time I watched it, whenever he caught that baby, I would well up. So glad I had the opportunity to get to know him. Not a mean bone in his body.'"

I thank David for what he did and Lupica for what he wrote. That was the Buckner I knew, and the treatment of him after that World Series was out of control. I was a David fan before, but I'm a bigger fan of David now because of what he did for Buckner while he was still alive to experience it. Buck said he had a lot of fun doing the show, and they treated him like they should have treated him, and he came away with a very positive experience from it. I felt like Buck not only was very grateful, but he was also relieved this major burden was somewhat lifted off his shoulders as they put him in a good light. They started concentrating on the good things that he was doing and they actually made him a hero in the show.

I knew a lot about Buckner before I ever met him. His older brother, Bobby, was with Tri-Cities, where I was assigned after being drafted, while Bill was sent to Ogden with all of the other draft picks. I was close with Bobby, and he kept me informed about his brother, who hit .344, .322, and .335 in three minor league seasons before making the big league club for good in 1971. Bill Buckner was a football and baseball star in high school in Napa. He had a baseball scholarship to USC but signed with the Los Angeles Dodgers and didn't play in college. Like me, Buckner had to attend school or be subject to the military draft and a likely assignment to Vietnam, so Buck went to class at USC, even though he wasn't playing on the USC baseball team, and then basic training. We were both late for spring training while serving our military commitment, and it wasn't until I showed up at Los Angeles International Airport that I met Buck. We sat and talked the whole time and got to know each other and then kind of felt like we were brothers when we got off the plane.

In Vero Beach, Florida, I hung with Buckner, Tom Paciorek, and Bobby Valentine. All four of us were multisport stars in high school, all very accomplished guys for our ages, and we formed a real strong friendship. Buck and I broke camp together and went to Double A Albuquerque. With him being from California and me from Washington, he had the better weather and was ahead of me conditioning-wise. I got off to a slow start, and our manager, Del Crandall, felt it would be better if I went to Single A Bakersfield to play for Ducky LeJohn, the same manager I had the year before at Tri-Cities. I had a really good year; Buckner did as well at Albuquerque, and after the season, we went to the Arizona Instructional League. Tommy Lasorda was our manager and pretty much was our mentor. During that time I can say that I saw something not many people have ever seen. I saw Lasorda pull a wallet out of his pocket and actually pay—not just for one meal—but for mine and Buck's too. It was at a smorgasbord called Sir George's. I think it cost $3 per person. Trust me: this group could eat, and we more than got Lasorda's money's worth. I'm not really sure how they stayed in business with the way we ate.

Buckner was a natural first baseman, but he was athletic enough to play the outfield, and that worked for him and against him. As he was coming up, it wasn't Steve Garvey who was being groomed to replace Wes Parker, a multi-Gold Glove first baseman. It was Buckner. But Von Joshua, who was our left fielder, broke his wrist in 1973. Buckner was asked if he would move to left field because that would open up first base for Garvey, whose auditions at third base and the outfield hadn't gone well. Buck was a tenacious outfielder, but he had chronic ankle problems that resulted in several operations. With Buckner's injuries limiting his outfield range, the Dodgers traded for Dusty Baker, who took over left field in 1976, moving Reggie Smith to right field, and the next year, the Dodgers dealt Buckner to the Chicago Cubs for Rick Monday, a natural center fielder.

Buckner was such a gamer. He played 15 years on that ruined ankle, and his pregame and postgame routine would make you cringe. He had both feet in a bucket of ice every single day before and after the game. I hated to see Buck traded to the Cubs. He was just a guy who was going to bust his ass for you every single day. If he hadn't had those physical issues, there's no telling how good he would have been. Buck went over to Chicago and mostly played first base for the Cubs. By then that was where he was best suited to play, and he was a pretty good first baseman.

I only spent a couple of years with him in L.A., and that was disappointing. But we ended up reuniting with the Cubs, and that turned out to be a really good thing. We spent a lot of time together in Chicago. His wife, Jody, and my wife, Fran, became friends. With the Cubs playing day games back then, we were able to socialize and actually could go home and eat dinner with the family. But that was just for 1983 because the Cubs turned first base over to Leon Durham in 1984, and Buck got traded to Boston.

One spring training at Vero Beach, Buck lived with us on the beach and he asked if I had a place to stay in L.A. yet. We didn't, and Buck said that was good because we'd live with him. He had a place off Malibu Canyon Road in the hills. It was 30 miles from the ballpark. I'm from a small town in the Northwest. That first year, I was constantly getting lost on the freeway. It was on the fringe of the San Fernando Valley, and back then the players either lived out there or out in Orange County. Doug Rau, Don Sutton, Garvey, Baker, Smith, Bill Russell, and Buckner all lived out in the Valley. Buckner got us out there first, and one Sunday, Fran and I got together with one of our pitchers, Pete Richert, for dinner at his house. And Richert asked me, "Do you know what one of the best things that you could do for yourself right now is? It's buy a house."

I started laughing. I couldn't afford that. I was in my early 20s, making $17,000. There's no way. It was a joke. It had to be a joke. And he said, "You're going to be here for a long time." I was two months away from finishing my rookie year, and buying a house was really not on my mind. I asked Richert what he knew that I didn't know. He said, "I just feel like you're gonna be here a long time."

I said, "Thank you so much for the confidence, but I don't know how that would work out."

But I figured Richert knew more than I did, so I told Fran she had carte blanche to start looking at homes. She narrowed it down to three homes, but we kept coming back to one in the hills just west of Topanga Canyon. I fell in love with it, and we bought it in September of 1973.

We still live in that house at the top of a canyon, almost 50 years later. When we moved in, you could only see a few houses in the canyon. Jamie Farr, one of the ensemble actors in the hit series *M*A*S*H*, lived in a home at the bottom of the canyon, and we used to yell to each other, and you could hear the echo through the canyon.

Buck came from Northern California wine country, but he wasn't California chill. Actually, back then you would have called him a red ass. He got upset when he made outs and he threw his bat and acted out a little bit. I did some of the same things but not to the degree that he did. For example, one day we came to the ballpark, and the lineup was posted, and he wasn't in it. Players want to play, and everybody reacts a little differently to the disappointment of not playing. On this day Buckner sulked like a little kid. When we took the field for batting practice, Buck sat down in left field. He was just sitting there while the rest of us were working. Walt Alston came out and went through his batting practice ritual. He walked behind the batting cage and started scanning around the field just to take inventory and he noticed a guy was sitting down in left field while everybody else out there was shagging—*because how could you not notice that?* And Alston, who was pretty mild-mannered but had a temper if pushed, went storming out to left field. Before he even got to Buck, he started yelling at him, telling him to get off the ground and be professional. Buck got up, and the two of them walked off the field and headed to the clubhouse. From the field you could hear them barking at each other. You couldn't make out exactly what they were saying, but it was pretty agitated. And the next thing you know, here came Buck running out of the tunnel and back into left field, and he's not sitting down anymore. So, you knew who won that argument.

There was a time when he didn't like hitting second so much because he'd have to hit behind guys who ran, and he had to try to pull the ball sometimes and move guys over. That's not the way they play today, but that's the kind of baseball we played. In fact, there was a time that no matter what place you hit in the lineup, when there was a guy on second base with fewer than two outs, it was expected that you hit the ball to the right side and moved the runner over. We had Davey Lopes getting on base, and you either let him steal second or you moved him over. That's why we had him. Buck, though, didn't like to give himself up so much. He could handle the bat. He could hit pitches over his head and hit pitches off his shoe tops. He could hit a pitch inside or outside. It didn't matter whether it was a ball or a strike; he'd find a way to make contact. You couldn't strike him out. His biggest asset was handling the bat. A lot like Rod Carew, he was able to hit the ball from line to line. And I remember him asking me once, "Which would you rather do? Would you rather hit .300 with 10 home runs or would you rather hit .270 with 25 home runs?"

I said, "Buck, you just described you and me. You're 10 and .300, I'm the other guy. They're not looking for me to hit 10 home runs and bat .300. They're looking for me to hit home runs and drive in runs. That's what they signed me to do. You can't do what I do, and I can't do what you do. Okay? So, I have to be me, and you have to be you. You're going to steal more bases than I and you're going to score more runs because I'm the guy who has to drive you in. I depend on you to get on base, and you depend on me to get you in. That's why I'm in the middle of the lineup."

Aside from the fact that we were friends, I admired his approach to the job. He was a gamer. Buckner could play for me anytime, anyplace, anywhere. This guy came to lace them up every single day. He always hustled, always played hard, gave up his body if needed. He was a ballplayer and he was my friend. RIP, Buck.

• CHAPTER 11 •

CUBBIES AND MANAGER RANTS

I sensed that my time in Los Angeles was about to come to an end, but the interesting thing was that the two clubs expressing the most interest in acquiring me in a trade, the White Sox and the Cubs, were in Fran's hometown of Chicago. With a possible homecoming for my wife on the table, it alleviated some of the anxiety about relocating from Los Angeles. Dallas Green, who was brought in from Philadelphia as general manager to end the Cubs' World Series drought and build a new tradition, not only worked out a trade for me after the 1982 season (for minor leaguers Dan Cataline and Vance Lovelace), but also treated me as a free agent, which was beyond generous. He tore up my contract with one year remaining and gave me a new five-year deal. Green eventually brought over a lot of players from the Philadelphia Phillies who had won the World Series in 1980, including Larry Bowa, Keith Moreland, Bob Dernier, Dickie Noles, Gary Matthews, Warren Brusstar, Dick Ruthven, Tim Stoddard, and Ryne Sandberg. Green knew what he wanted to do and was given the freedom by the new Tribune Company ownership to do it. He wanted to win right away and had new money to spend. I played against Green and I liked him. I knew that he could be difficult, hard on his players. Philadelphia, after all, was a difficult city to play in. Phillies fans booed their best players quite a bit, which they almost never did in Los Angeles. When we would have a rocky spell in L.A., fans treated us pretty much like family. It was like, "We don't need to send the kids off to the room. Let's just let them calm down. Don't punish them; don't make it any worse than it needs to be." We had a track record, and everybody knew we'd recover and be fine. That's not how fans were in Philadelphia or Chicago.

We got creative with the contract to minimize some of Green's issues with me being "overpaid." There was concern that a big contract for a new player might rock the boat a little bit. He and Steve Schneider, my attorney, came up with a Wrigley Field-related attendance clause. It was a roll of the dice for me because it wasn't guaranteed and it was a little touch-and-go in the beginning. At the end of my first year there, we came within 20,000 tickets of reaching the first part of my bonus for attendance. And I knew if we won, more fans would come, and a positive byproduct would be that my bonus would kick in. And, sure enough, along came 1984.

When the Cubs brought me over, it wasn't only to play third base. Green told me he wanted me to lead and to bring some of the winning Dodgers attitude into the clubhouse. He wanted a highly competitive team. My first spring training, we were going to play the San Francisco Giants in Scottsdale, Arizona. When you travel in spring training, as you're getting off the bus, the driver unloads all of the equipment bags from the underneath storage compartment and lays them next to the bus on the pavement, and every player grabs a bag and carries it into the clubhouse—even if it's not his bag. Sharing the workload like that is just baseball tradition and part of being a good teammate. So, I got off the bus and saw the driver laying out the bags. There was an Oakland A's bag. There was a Philly bag. There's a New York Mets bag, a Giants bag, a Pittsburgh Pirates bag, a San Diego Padres bag, and a Los Angeles Dodgers bag. And I was thinking, *What are we? A co-op team.* It just bothered me that we looked so ragtag. When I got back after the game, I left a message for Green that I wanted to talk to him. I told him what I saw the day before and how I felt. If we were going to establish a new team identity, we needed to do that immediately. We needed to start being known as the Chicago Cubs, not a collection of players from around baseball. He was very receptive to it. He said, "I don't know how this kind of slipped past me, but you're 100 percent right."

The Cubs clubhouse manager was the legendary Yosh Kawano, coincidentally the brother of longtime Dodgers clubhouse manager Nobe Kawano. As I got to know Yosh, I learned that he was more outgoing than Nobe. Yosh was usually yucking it up, keeping everybody loose. But the day after my meeting with Green, Yosh wasn't laughing. He was huffing and puffing about how all the bright and shiny new Cubs equipment bags needed to be rolled out for Opening Day. He was getting this rant out because all these bags he had tucked away were on stools in front of our lockers. Yosh's protests aside, Green used to tell that story about our new bags fondly. He'd say, "I brought this guy over here for reasons that I probably couldn't have explained to you at all. But when you talk about having a person who's been there, who has had a leadership role, and then you see where this comes from, this is good. We're being united here. This is what I wanted. I didn't know how it was going to happen, when it was going to happen, or what it was going to be about, but this is exactly what I need from these guys, this kind of insight."

Of course, you don't win a pennant with an equipment bag, but I was already feeling good about the way Green had improved the roster. He upgraded the condition of the home clubhouse in a big way. It was almost state of the art compared to the old, cramped clubhouse. We had a weight room, an enlarged training room, everything we needed. It made a difference and it also became a lure for free agents. They want to be coming into a facility that will help them be the best they can be. They don't want to go back in time with a clubhouse that hasn't changed in 30 or 40 years, which was the case at Wrigley Field until they built this new one.

After a couple of months, I got a call from Green saying, "I have an opportunity to get a guy that you know very well. I want your opinion on Rick Sutcliffe."

Sut and I were teammates with the Dodgers, and I gave Green a thumbs up. I said, "This is a guy who won 17 games his rookie year. He's a bulldog, he can even swing the bat a little bit. He's durable. He's a guy that's gonna be your ace. If you have a chance to get him, I would say do it."

So Sutcliffe came over and won 16 of 17 decisions and made me look a lot better in the eyes of management. And Sutcliffe made our pitching staff very comparable to everyone else, including the Mets. We took Chicago by storm. They didn't know what to do with themselves when we got to September because they hadn't experienced this in four decades. Almost daily, the media would be asking questions like, "Is this really going to happen?"

I wasn't making any predictions, but I said I'd been through this quite a few times before and I felt really good about our chances. We were playing well, we were healthy, and we had a nice, comfortable lead. The next day, I'd get asked the same question, and it was the same thing day after day until we finally clinched the thing. We had a pretty significant celebration because we had a major opportunity to end this drought for the Cubs. We were going to play San Diego for the pennant, and I thought we really matched up well. I also thought we matched up well with the Detroit Tigers, who eventually went on to win the World Series against San Diego.

Instead, we gave away the series to the Padres. We made one very big mistake in that series, and I'm not talking about Leon Durham. With a 2–1 lead in the series, we had a chance to close it out in Game Four. It was Sutcliffe's turn to start. But management got greedy. The decision was made to start Scott Sanderson instead. The explanation was that if we won Game Four with Sanderson, we had Sutcliffe to open the World Series. And if we lost Game Four, we would still have Sutcliffe for Game Five. When Sarge (Matthews) told me they were switching Game Four starters, I said, "You can't really do this."

I really felt it was a huge mistake. Put your best guy out there and close it out. Don't worry about the next series. But they decided to flip it. Sanderson had been rehabbing, and this was like his first game in a month. And it's not that he pitched poorly. It's just the psychology of what we did. If we send Sutcliffe out there to shut the door, we're saying to the opponent, "Beat this guy that shut you out in the first game. Go ahead." But when they flipped it, we're saying, "We're actually going to give you an opportunity to play a Game Five," and that's exactly what happened. If you've been around long enough, anyone will tell you that anything can happen in an all-or-nothing game. You can have your best pitcher out there, but it's still not going to be an easy game.

And we know what happened. We lost the lead in the seventh inning of Game Five, a ground ball went through Durham's legs at first base, and the Cubs' World Series drought continued. This was my second all-time worst defeat. The first one was the '78 World Series, and this one, though it's a notch down on the scale, shouldn't have happened either. It was self-inflicted. The Sanderson decision was made by manager Jim Frey. In today's game it would never happen like that. Now the front office has a lot of say in these decisions. They run the data through the algorithms, and analytics spits out the probabilities. But back then the general manager usually gave the manager authority for those decisions.

In that 1984 season, I hurt both wrists. I got hit by a pitch on the right wrist and needed to wear a protective pad. On certain pitches inside, it really hurt, and I had a hard time dealing with it. As I was starting to get it together after that, I was chasing a foul ball down the line in Cincinnati and dove for the ball. My glove kind of buckled my left wrist, and I popped something in my wrist. I had to wrap both of my wrists but still ended up hitting 25 home runs and driving in 97 runs. But in the playoffs, I was hurt again, and this one was completely avoidable. This one was literally another self-inflicted wound. I tweaked my right elbow carrying my luggage on the road. That was the only time I had ever done that in my entire career; I should have just left it for the bellman to bring it up to the room. It was just one of those things where I was carrying it awkwardly for a period of time and it just kind of locked up. And it happened at such an important time of our season. We didn't announce it, and I tried to play around it, but I couldn't straighten out that arm.

We had a really good infield with the Cubs. Bowa was the shortstop, and if he wasn't a Hall of Famer, he was right on the edge defensively. Sandberg, the second baseman, is in the Hall of Fame. Sandberg was a great fielder but an unconventional one. Unlike guys like Bill Mazeroski and Joe Morgan and Davey Lopes, he had an awkward style of reaching for ground balls instead of gently allowing the ball to come to him. It was unorthodox, but he could make all the plays.

While I was in Chicago, Shawon Dunston came up to replace Bowa at shortstop. My son hung with Dunston a lot, and I got to know him as well as I did any of the young Cubs. He was just a great talent. And he was famous for his arm. He had the strongest arm of any shortstop

I ever played with—maybe, if possible, too good of an arm. He was absolutely killing Durham over at first base with one-hoppers off his shins or he'd air mail throws 10 rows into the stands. I tried to help him harness that. I said, "Shawon, you don't need to show off your arm on every play. Save it for the bang-bang play." Most of the time, it's just catch and release. That's what Ozzie Smith and Brooks Robinson did, and they won Gold Gloves every year. It was almost like he was still trying to impress the scouts.

Once we were able to harness that, Dunston did a much better job. Harnessing it, though, required some remedial instruction. The story I tell is that I was warming up with him in spring training one morning, and every throw of his came with a different rotation on it. As an infielder you want to have a four-seam grip because it carries better. It comes to the first baseman accurately and without fading or sinking; most of all, it's consistent. So I called timeout. I said, "Shawon, what are you doing?"

And he said, "What do you mean?"

I said, "Every ball that you're throwing to me has a different rotation. Just throw a four-seamer."

He said, "Do what?"

And I said, "You mean to tell me that you're in the major leagues for a year, and nobody has taught you the proper grip on a baseball for an infielder?"

So I showed him how to grip the ball, how to spin it around in his hand to manipulate the seams so it would be in the right place when he releases it. I couldn't believe that I was teaching him things he should have learned his very first spring training. But maybe because his arm was so powerful, nobody ever stopped to ask if he was doing it correctly.

Although 1984 ended in disappointment, everything looked bright regarding our roster and clubhouse. We started off the next year playing well and were in first place by June. We were healthy and right where we wanted to be, and guys said how good it felt. It was like we had recovered from the hangover of the playoff loss, and we were moving forward. Then, as happens to every team, we had a rash of injuries. We lost our entire starting pitching rotation, started to struggle, and then couldn't score enough runs. And we didn't have anyone who was able to come in and replace these guys. We really went in the tank, and things progressively got worse. And this was right about the time everyone's kids were getting out of school for the summer and were all coming to Chicago. About two days before they came in, Frey made about the worst decision he could have made, considering the situation. Because we were playing so poorly, he told us there wouldn't be any kids allowed in the clubhouse. I mean, he was going to punish us. And there were about 25 guys who wanted to rip his head off. If anything, the kids would have given us a little bit of a lift. That's what we all thought. Nobody was happy about it, but Moreland literally had to be held down because he was ready to charge the guy. Eventually, we got past it, but it's an example of what can happen to the chemistry of a team and how a manager can over-think things sometimes. Prohibiting kids in the clubhouse wasn't going to make anything better.

Personally, Frey's insensitivity was so contrary to what I had experienced with the Dodgers, where everybody really was part of a family. The team was owned by a family, the O'Malleys. Kids were always around. Tommy Lasorda knew every one of them by their first name, and I'm not exaggerating. "I love my Uncle Tommy," he would implore the kids to recite when they would come running into his clubhouse office. The Dodgers threw Christmas parties for the kids at Dodgertown every spring training. They had fake snow, Santa Claus, and gift-wrapped presents for all. Of course, the Dodgers really were an outlier in a lot of ways. We had our own plane. We had the best attendance. We had a farm system that kept the talent coming. To the rest of the game, we were spoiled. And beyond the obvious benefits, there were probably edges that we had over other teams before the game even started. I think that gave us a psychological edge. I don't know that opponents were envious of us, but I know we felt like we lived in a penthouse. I'm not saying that to rub it in, but we weren't staying in modest hotels on the road; we had the suite. We weren't flying commercial; we were flying the Kay O' II with the Dodgers logo on the fuselage. We were living better, eating better, and training in better facilities. And if you get somebody thinking that way, that's obviously to your advantage. But there's also the flip side. We didn't sneak up on anybody. Opponents would come at us a little bit harder to take us off this pedestal. This was confirmed any time a player from another club joined the Dodgers in a trade or as a free agent. We would hear the stories of how much we were disliked. I don't think our players necessarily felt superior in that regard. We just knew we were the Dodgers organization, a step above most everybody else on all levels—even if that put a target on our back.

Of course, part of our reputation bordered on the absurd. Having played for Lasorda, I was familiar with a manager going berserk with the media. Lasorda had one of the most famous sports meltdowns of all time after a Mother's Day game against the Cubs at Dodger Stadium in 1978. Dave Kingman hit three home runs against us, and we lost 10–7 in 15 innings. And after the game, a young radio stringer named Paul Olden kneeled down next to Lasorda in his office, put a microphone in front of Lasorda, and innocently asked a seemingly logical, straightforward question: "What did you think of Kingman's performance?"

Without even raising his voice, Lasorda unleashed an epic, profane rant:

"What's my opinion of Kingman's performance? What the fuck do you think my opinion is? I think it was fucking horseshit. Put that in. I don't fucking care. What's my opinion of his performance? Jesus Christ, he beat us with three fucking home runs. What the fuck do you mean, 'What is my opinion of his performance?' How can you ask me a question like that: my opinion of his performance? Jesus Christ, I'm pissed off because we lost the fucking game. And you asked me my opinion of his performance. Jesus Christ, that's a tough question to ask me, 'What is my opinion of his performance?' I didn't give you a good answer because I'm mad. But I mean, it wasn't a good question. It's a tough question to ask me right now. What is my opinion of his performance? I mean, you want me to tell you what my opinion of his performance is. Jesus Christ, he hit three home runs against us. I mean, I don't want to get pissed off or anything like that. But you know you asked me my opinion. He put on a hell of a show. He hit three home runs, he drove in, what, seven runs? Eight? What the hell more can you say about it?"

It went on and on like that, but because it was on tape, the public got a rare view of what we had been hearing since instructional league. In fact, Lasorda was so proficient unleashing expletives that Rick Monday took it upon himself to count them each and every time Lasorda went off at us in team meetings. Monday had one of those handheld tally counters the pitching coaches use to count pitches. Instead, Monday would be clicking away counting Lasorda expletives. And when the meeting was over and Lasorda left the clubhouse, everybody would look at Monday for a thumbs-up that would verify whether Lasorda had set another personal record for F-bombs. I'm sure Lasorda believed that his salty language would touch a nerve and inspire us to do better. In actuality, we thought it was hilarious. And it probably had the intended effect in an indirect way. It cut the tension because it was so funny.

I figured I would never again hear anything publicly like Lasorda's rampage. But during my first year with the Cubs in 1983, I heard even worse from our manager, Lee Elia. He went off on Cubs fans like few managers ever had before him and none since. I must admit that it was sort of because of me. Here's why. After signing a five-year contract, I had a great spring training, like the best one I've ever had, and I was ready to go. We opened the season in Chicago. We were getting ready for Opening Day introductions out on the baseline, and it was absolutely freezing. As soon as the intros were over, the game was canceled. We had 35,000 people in the stands, but it was snowing. The next day we were able to play, but only 5,000 people showed up. I hit rockets my first home-stand as a Cubs player with nothing to show for it. We got snowed out in Philadelphia and we got bad weather like usual in Pittsburgh—freezing weather, just horrible throughout. By the end of May, I was hitting maybe .150 with maybe one home run. I hurt my shoulder, but I was playing with it and I probably made eight of my 13 errors that year in April. And it wasn't until June when things started to heat up. And then from that point on, it became a .275 average/24-homer/90-RBIs season and it ended up being okay. But that start was miserable. I couldn't do anything right. Even when I hit a ball well, somebody would make a play.

Elia was the one who was kind of standing up for me at that point in time, but he was getting tired of hearing about it from the fans. So, of course, the Dodgers were in town April 29, and I was struggling, and we lost a one-run game to the Dodgers, and it was just a perfect storm. The fans were brutal the whole game—and especially as we came off the field after losing to the Dodgers. Speaking with reporters in his office after the game, Elia was asked about the fans booing his players. Among the many unwritten rules in sports is never, ever take a shot at the fans. They are our customers, they're paying our salaries, and even if it's bad form, they are entitled to voice their displeasure by booing. Elia knew the drill; he wasn't a rookie. He had been a player, coach, manager, and scout. But he couldn't control himself and went absolutely batshit, and the late Les Grobstein from radio station WLS AM had the only microphone in the room to record it for posterity:

"Fuck those fucking fans who come out here and say they're Cub fans that are supposed to be behind you, rippin' every fucking thing you do, I'll tell you one fucking thing, I hope we get fucking hotter than shit, just to stuff it up them 3,000 fucking people that show up every fucking day because if they're the real Chicago fucking fans, they can kiss my fucking ass right downtown and *print it*. They're really, really behind you around here...my fucking ass. What the fuck am I supposed to do? Go out there and let my fucking players get destroyed every day and be quiet about it? For the fucking nickel-dime people who turn up? The motherfuckers don't even work. That's why they're out at the [expletive] game. They oughta go out and get a fucking job and find out what it's like to go out and earn a fucking living. Eighty-five percent of the fucking world is working. The other 15 percent come out here, a fucking playground for the cocksuckers. Rip them motherfuckers. Rip them fuckin' cocksuckers like the fuckin' players. We got guys bustin' their fuckin' ass, and them fucking people boo. And that's the Cubs? My players get around here. They talk about the great fucking support the players get around here. I haven't seen it this fucking year. Everybody associated with this organization have been winners their whole fucking life, everybody. And the credit is not given in that respect.

"All right, they don't show because we're 5–14...and unfortunately, that's the criteria of them dumb 15 motherfucking percent that come out to day baseball. The other 85 percent are earning a living. I tell you, it'll take more than a 5–12 or 5–14 to destroy the makeup of this club. I guarantee you that. There's some fucking pros out there that wanna win. But you're stuck in a fucking stigma of the fucking Dodgers and the Phillies and the Cardinals and all that cheap shit. It's unbelievable. It really is. It's a disheartening fucking situation that we're in right now. Anybody who was associated with the Cub organization four or five years ago that came back and sees the multitude of progress that's been made will understand that if they're baseball people, that 5–14 doesn't negate all that work. We got 143 fucking games left.

"What I'm tryin' to say is don't rip them fucking guys out there. Rip me. If you wanna rip somebody, rip my fucking ass. But don't rip them fucking guys 'cause they're givin' everything they can give. And right now they're tryin' to do more than God gave 'em, and that's why we make the simple mistakes. That's exactly why."

If Monday had been in that clubhouse counting F-bombs, his pitch counter would have overheated. It might sound ridiculous, but I truly believe Elia didn't mean to insult the fans. He was defending his players. His heart was in the right place, but the execution was a mess—just like Lasorda on the Kingman thing. Lasorda's interview became comical, and there really wasn't any fallout. Elia's tirade targeted the fans, and that's a line you just can't cross. I don't think they ever forgave him.

Of course, no interview during my playing days had the impact of the Al Campanis *Nightline* interview. When asked by Ted Koppel about the lack of African Americans in high-ranking Major League Baseball positions, Campanis said, "I don't believe it's prejudice. I truly believe that they may not have some of the necessities to be, let's say, a field manager or perhaps a general manager." He went on to make ignorant comments about why Blacks were not suited to be swimmers, pitchers, or quarterbacks.

I was no longer with the club when that went down. I had had my share of issues with Campanis when he was the Dodgers general manager. But when the *Nightline* interview happened, I was with the A's, and we were in Minnesota. Reggie Jackson was on my team for his final season before retiring. He had been contacted by the media to comment on Campanis and he came to me first, asking if I would consider Campanis a racist because of all my dealings with him. I told

Jackson that there was no way Campanis is a racist. I wasn't his biggest fan after some of the things he did to me, but there's no way that he meant it to sound the way that it did. I know that he got stuck in the conversation. I know that they offered him a way out. And for some reason he didn't see it and went past it and said what he said. But I told Jackson that when you think about the Dodgers heritage, history, and tradition and you bring up Jackie Robinson and all the other Black players that we had, Campanis was right there with Robinson, helping him learn the intricacies of playing second base and supporting him off the field. Campanis was the biggest reason the Dodgers were so successful signing players from the Caribbean. He didn't care what color you were or where you came from as long as you had baseball talent. There wasn't any racism in Campanis. There might have been ignorance because of the way he was raised, but he wasn't a bigot. Campanis and Robinson were friends. The Dodgers were in the forefront of bringing everybody and anybody into the game, no matter your background. Not just Robinson, but Hideo Nomo, Chan Ho Park, Fernando Valenzuela, all the Caribbean players. I understand why the reaction to Campanis' words were swift and strong, but it's also a shame that his contributions to the Dodgers organization and the game seem to have been stricken from the record.

While I wish the Dodgers had been a little kinder to Campanis in his later years, I can't complain about my treatment once I left. When I returned to Dodger Stadium for the first time as a Cubs player in 1983, they honored me with Ron Cey Night. I was looking forward to that night, but there was also a little bit of animosity in me. I walked on the field to take our batting practice and I was walking out to third base, and Lasorda was on the top step of the Dodgers' dugout. As I walked by, he said, "Well, are you going to say hi?"

And I said, "Well, are you going to say hi?" So, we went over and embraced, and later he was part of the ceremony.

But it's the old saying, "It's not personal; it's just business." If you're able to accept that concept, it makes it a lot easier to move on because that essentially is kind of how it works. It's kind of like corporate America in the same sense. I get it, but I felt like Lasorda could have smoothed it over a little bit better for me. I tried to let it go so I could move on.

Coming back to Dodger Stadium, getting a standing ovation, having the fans show appreciation for what I had done was a very special time. Getting used to wearing a different uniform, different number, and somewhat different expectations was challenging, but I felt the Cubs were on the rise. I didn't want to go to a place where I was just eating up time. I had learned the game and I wanted something to play for every day. I wanted to win. I wanted to show them that I had something left, that they traded me too early. I think that is a probably normal thought that players have.

They moved me out so Pedro Guerrero could play third base, but Guerrero couldn't play third base. Lasorda would tell the story about Guerrero having a tough time at third base. When he asked Guerrero what he was thinking as he's playing third base, Guerrero said, "Well, I'm thinking about I don't want them to hit the ball to me anymore."

And Lasorda said, "Anything else?"

And Guerrero said, "Yeah, I don't want them to hit the ball to [Steve Sax] either."

I thought this was the greatest response to a question that I've ever heard simply because he defused the whole situation. I thought it was brilliant. I really did. The fact that he added Saxy to it was hysterical.

After four years with the Cubs and with one year remaining on my contract, I went through the same youth movement I experienced with the Dodgers, but this time I was 39 years old. The Cubs wanted to move Moreland to third base, and the designated hitter rule made a move to the American League for me understandable. A few weeks before spring training, I was traded to Oakland for Luis Quinones, a utilityman who played for five major league clubs. It turned out to be a very uncomfortable move for me. I was trying to cope with a new mental approach, sitting around for a half hour after each at-bat without playing defense. I spoke to a few other veterans who had done it, and our hitting coach was Bob Watson, who was with the New York Yankees when we beat them in the World Series. Watson was an astute guy and he helped me as much as he could. But I wasn't playing third base with Carney Lansford there and I wasn't playing first base with a young Mark McGwire breaking through. I was just trying to find some spots where I could fit in. But it was too hard to stay sharp. Everybody retires at some point, and I was starting to feel like I had a really long career. I was disappointed that I couldn't get this DH job done, but it just didn't work out. On July 15, 1987, I was released by the A's and began my retirement from being an active Major League Baseball player.

• CHAPTER 12 •

BEST OWNERS

I was very lucky to play for the O'Malley family because they don't make owners like that anymore. From operating a Dodgertown spring training complex that was the envy of baseball to privately-funded Dodger Stadium nestled in Chavez Ravine to the perk of flying a private airplane fitted with first-class accommodations throughout, the O'Malleys were a throwback to the days when families, and not corporations, owned baseball teams. The O'Malleys considered themselves stewards of a public trust and treated players like part of their family. Walter O'Malley, who gained full control of the club in 1950, groomed his son, Peter, to take over the daily operation of the business, which he did in 1970. After Walter died in 1979, Peter ran the club and owned it in partnership with his sister, Terry, keeping it in the family nearly two more decades. But with deep-pocket conglomerates buying up clubs and also being blocked by local politicians from building a football stadium to lure an NFL team, the O'Malleys decided they couldn't compete financially and sold the club to Rupert Murdoch's News Corp. in 1997 for $310 million. It was probably the right move for the O'Malleys, even though it meant the end of stability for a franchise built upon it. It also can be said, in hindsight, that they sold low. Seven years after buying the club primarily to provide programming for its regional sports network, News Corp. sold the Dodgers to Bostonian Frank McCourt for $421 million. Eight years after that, a coalition backed by private equity investors Guggenheim Partners and including iconic frontman Magic Johnson bought the Dodgers out of bankruptcy for $2 billion.

I had a unique relationship with the O'Malleys, and it dated to an unexpected encounter during my first spring training in Vero Beach, Florida. Dodgertown originally was an abandoned naval air station, and the players lived in the original barracks, which had only overhead fans to combat the searing Florida weather, community showers, and one phone that we had to wait in line to use. Dodgertown was a comfortable facility for the executives, but it was not a country club for the minor leaguers. On one particularly hot and humid night, Bobby Valentine and I decided to walk from the barracks to where the big swimming pool was, just outside of the cabanas near the basketball and tennis courts. I'm not sure we realized it at the time, but these amenities were clustered around the cabanas where the O'Malley family spent spring training. We were just trying to cool off by the pool on a hot night because we really couldn't sleep. Maybe we were talking a little too loud or maybe we weren't the only ones having trouble sleeping, but we heard this froggy voice asking who was out there. We couldn't see who was talking because there was glare from a big spotlight that was aimed at the pool. But as he emerged, we realized the speaker was owner Walter O'Malley, whose rough voice was the result of throat cancer. Mr. O'Malley sat with us for probably an hour, just talking about things in general. I might have been 21, a minor leaguer, and here was Walter O'Malley, lawyer, engineer, and owner of the Los Angeles Dodgers. We were out of our league, but he didn't make us feel out of place, not at all. If anything, we actually felt like we were really lucky to be able to have some time with the owner. He was just trying to get to know us, get some background on us. It was very cool. Even at the time, I felt like that was a moment that I would always remember. Honestly, how many owners are going to take the time to come out and talk to two kids who have just been signed, who are trying to fight their way through this minor league system, and who eventually become Major League Baseball players? That showed us what the O'Malley family really was all about. I think a lot of owners are wearing suits and acting important, and it gets a little stuffy. Not the O'Malleys.

Walter died in 1979 and was elected into the Hall of Fame in 2008, and I don't understand why it took that long. That was 50 years after he orchestrated baseball's move to the West Coast, convincing the Giants to also leave New York so the Dodgers wouldn't be flying solo into the new frontier. Now there are 11 teams west of St. Louis, but until O'Malley made the move, there was none. It was O'Malley who had the vision, who played the necessary city politics, who financed and built his own stadium. He was villainized for leaving Brooklyn, but he brought a lot of employees with him, and many of them continued to work for the club, including Vin Scully, who topped that list for decades.

One of the things that I really enjoyed about the organization was the way they treated minor leaguers. When you went into the clubhouse as a minor league player, there weren't any "Do Not Enter" signs, there wasn't an attitude that you weren't yet worthy of walking into the clubhouse, which I had heard from friends who found that to be the case with other organizations. You shouldn't put the sacred place off-limits. It's kind of a shrine to the kids who are coming up, and they should be encouraged to walk through those doors. I wanted to be able to talk to those guys and feel at home. We did, and it was fun being able to go into the clubhouse and just sit around with those guys and talk a little bit. For my first full spring training, I was on the 40-man roster with a locker in the major league clubhouse, and that felt really good. Even though I wasn't really a part of that club on the field, it was nice to have your locker in there.

It's a feeling of progress subliminally, and then I went to work out with these guys, and it just made it more relaxed. I wanted to make sure that my locker was in there from here on out. This is where the great teams and the great players before you were, and obviously you want to have your team picture and your own picture up on the wall and be a part of this history and tradition. And every time I spoke to any kids after that, my message was, "You've got to want to be that guy whose picture is on that wall. You've got to want to have your teams up there, too. This is what you're playing for. This is it. You're not coming into just another organization here. This is what we expect. We want the best out of you."

Of all the perks, it was the private team plane—The Kay O' II named after Walter O'Malley's wife—that really set us apart. And it wasn't just an elitist statement. It was a functional advantage. Like any team, we're on the road half of the season. And a dedicated private plane made traveling as convenient and comfortable as possible. For obvious reasons, it was the envy of every other club, but it really was a blessing because we saved a lot of hours by being able to get in and out as quickly as we did. Our pilot, Lew Carlisle, was able to divert around storms, and we never seemed to get stuck on runways or at gates. It was like we had the FASTPASS at Disneyland. It was like he was in control of the control tower. The Dodgers name had clout. It was definitely an asset and it was a lot of fun. Lew's wife, Millie, was the flight attendant. They knew every Dodgers player from the day they arrived and they treated us like guests in their home. Our meals were better than those on commercial flights. We got to sit up in the cockpit at times and get a view of what it's like up there while chatting with Lew and his copilot, Frank Fleischmann, better known as "Fan Jet." They were fun, great people and they were always happy for us. It was a mutual relationship thing that worked really well. I'm really happy that I was part of it.

Another aspect to the way the O'Malleys ran the team was their respect for the sanctity of the clubhouse. You never saw Walter O'Malley or Peter O'Malley down there unless there was a monumental reason like the awarding of the World Series trophy. The O'Malleys believed in a separation of the front office and the clubhouse like the separation of church and state. That, I thought, was really respectful. Even though they owned the place, they always knew their place. Their seats were always up by the press box—not in the front row by the field. This wasn't about them. They let us just do our job. The O'Malleys would never come down and start throwing tantrums like George Steinbrenner was known to do with the New York Yankees. The O'Malleys left it to the players and manager to work our stuff out when things were bad and to relish the wins when they came. That doesn't mean they were disengaged. I know for a fact that Peter privately wore those games on his sleeve. We would hear about it. People would say, "Peter's not necessarily in a great mood today."

But he never created an uncomfortable situation. Maybe that was Peter's way because it was Walter's way, but remember that Peter worked his way up. He ran Dodgertown. He was general manager of our Triple A team. He learned the business from the ground up. I think that's the best way to prepare for sitting in the main seat. Because of his training, Peter seemed to have a greater understanding and appreciation of all the employees, including the players. We had to work our way up like he did. I wasn't always flying on the team plane. I had those long, uncomfortable bus trips like everybody else did. The one from Lewiston, Idaho to Medford, Oregon, took about 15 hours but felt like three days. And it wasn't one of those comfortable Greyhound coaches; it was more like a used school bus that's going about 45 miles an hour. We were given $3 a day for meal money. That's why Tommy Lasorda cultivated relationships with restaurant owners: to get his players fed. And as miserable as it seemed at the time, I'm glad I experienced all of it. I felt like I paid my dues. I got to live in the old barracks at Dodgertown. Then I saw the new renovations, the new Dodgertown. It was a process, and I enjoyed being a part of it instead of just coming in and hearing about it. There wasn't somebody handing you the keys to the car and your house. I'm glad I had a chance to go through the stages like those before me. It's only natural to want to take shortcuts at times, but there are other times when you really kind of need to go through the whole process. It's like grades one through 12. You don't want to start skipping stuff because it leaves holes in the foundation. I think you learn it better and I think you appreciate it better the way we did it.

The O'Malleys also treated the players' family like family. I remember when Peter's wife, Annette, decided to treat the Dodgers wives, who came to spring training, for a spa day. But it wasn't a spa day in Vero Beach, a spa day in Florida, or even a spa day in the United States. She borrowed the team plane and flew all the wives to the Bahamas for a spa day at a resort. Talk about extending yourself and being friendly. This is why the O'Malleys were so loved by everyone that worked for them. They also threw a Christmas party at Dodgertown every spring so they could celebrate the holiday with all of the families. They brought in snow for kids, handed out gifts, and it was just an amazing time.

Peter also felt it was important to keep former players in the organization—a win for the retired player, the fans, and the club's public image. If you look back at the money that was being paid to players of my generation, it was paltry. For example, in my rookie season, it was $13,500. I could have made that much working at my dad's gas station. Now the minimum is $700,000. That's not the average; it's the minimum. I shake my head and just start laughing at that number and wish I had been born 50 years later. Obviously, the money was not a lure in my time, not remotely. And it wasn't until free agency and arbitration took hold that players received an equitable piece of the golden pie. Everybody kind of knew that there was a lot of money down in the vault, and we opened that up and brought it to the top and owners had to share.

As for dealing with players as labor, Peter went along with the other owners as far as the pay scale for active players, but taking care of the former players—and I'm included in that as much as anybody—didn't take a backseat. A few years after I retired, he offered me a position with the club that I held for more than 25 years. He gave me an opportunity to get back into the game and be a little more visible. Peter gave me free rein to create a position, and that took a while. Over the years I've worn many hats—more on the business side than the baseball side. I was long a part of the luxury suite program. When seating areas on the press level were converted into 30 suites during the News Corp ownership, Bob Daly, the former studio executive who had become club president, had me entertaining entertainers who would visit. Additionally, I've done meet-and-greets with clients and prospective clients for suite sales. I took it upon myself to show up with memorabilia, autographed balls, programs, game notes, and stats from the press box, anything I felt would make future suite holders feel like insiders. Kris Rone, my supervisor at the time, thanked me for making it a better experience and gave me a raise. I felt I was just doing my job. Since then, the role evolved into more courtesy visits, where I stopped in to check on the suite holders, helping manage those relationships and appearing whenever a salesperson asked. I've also represented the club at the MLB draft at MLB Network's Studio 42, including the time I went with Lasorda but didn't come back with him. That was the draft when Lasorda suffered a heart attack in the draft room. Commissioner Bud Selig and another former Dodgers manager, Joe Torre, had to convince Lasorda to go to the hospital. It was a tough sell. Lasorda finally agreed and he was there for three or four days before they released him. Another one of my duties was to participate in spring training as a guest instructor. I also set up the program to bring in other former players—both from my generation and more recently retired players—as guest instructors.

Before rejoining the Dodgers, I did some broadcasting of Dodgers games on an early version of regional pay-per-view. It was a way to get my feet wet and see if an analyst role suited me. We did 35 games, and veteran broadcaster Joel Meyers was the play-by-play man. It worked for me because it was all home games, so I didn't have to travel after being on the road so much while playing. I got to learn the business. Looking back on it, I probably would have done things a little differently. At the time I felt that my baseball experience would carry me and I would comment on what I saw each game. But there were times the producer would ask me to talk about games I hadn't covered, and they clearly were expecting me to have watched every play of every inning of every game whether I was covering it or not. My focus had been on that specific game, and they wanted more of a full-time dedication to it. I'm glad I had the experience, but I don't regret moving on. I wasn't really ready to make that kind of a commitment. The Dodgers have really changed their approach on that in recent years, especially after Scully retired. Now they have a long roster of analysts who they shuffle in and out, and there aren't the same expectations. It's better suited now to the former player who really wants a part-time job. With the money made by recently retired players, it's unrealistic to expect a big-name player to accept the travel demands of a full-time gig. When you're a Dodgers broadcaster doing all the home games and all the road games, that's like playing the game out of uniform.

• CHAPTER 13 •

Marvin Miller
and the Business of Baseball

Eight years after he died, 38 years after he retired, and 46 years after he won free agency for Major League Baseball players, Marvin Miller was voted into the Hall of Fame. What took so long? Miller, the executive director of the Major League Baseball Players Association from 1966 to 1982, guided our union from a powerless group of underpaid entertainers to a collective bargaining powerhouse, winning legal and labor battles that supercharged increases in salaries, pension funds, and licensing rights.

Because of that he is owed an immense debt of gratitude by just about every guy who has worn a major league uniform in the last half century and every player going forward. The benefits that today's players enjoy—the mega-salaries, the pension, the health coverage, generous meal money, and first-class accommodations—exist because of Miller. He never tried to take credit for it. He would always say, "It wasn't just me. It was because you guys held together and went on strike and did all that fighting."

Maybe so, but it wasn't until Miller led the union that we made any progress. Every army needs a general, and every company needs a strong CEO if you want the whole to be greater than the sum of its parts. Miller was the heart and soul of this whole thing. His background was that of a negotiator for the steelworkers' union in Pittsburgh, so he knew how to gain concessions from tough owners. We had to trust him, his experience, his knowledge. He seemed to be very thorough, very calm, very assured. He never got ruffled. I just trusted his demeanor and I liked him from the beginning. It wasn't one of those things where I grew to like him, or I overcame some of the things that he was short on. He had the qualifications. He was skilled at passing on information to us. We had player reps, but none of them was an experienced professional labor leader like him. He gained the players' trust by always explaining the issues to us and answering every question.

When we met with him individually, Miller was always straightforward. I felt we were in really good hands. I did not feel that there was anything but an overwhelming majority of support every time. There might have been a few guys who had some questions about this or were unhappy about that, but it wasn't going to tilt anything in the wrong direction. The one thing I concluded when Miller made his rounds to brief each team was that his main objective was to keep the players united. He always told us, "We'll outlast them." He sensed that as hard as it might be to keep 750 players pulling in the same direction, it would be harder to keep 26 wealthy owners in synch. That math might not make sense on the surface, but he was right. He would say, "We can't have divided factions here. We need to stay together, and if we do stay together, we will win, and you will come away winners."

And my opinion was that we did come away with the most important bullet points. Maybe we didn't win as much as we had wanted to win, but we came out with pretty much the things that mattered most, the real meat and potatoes like free agency, pension increases, and arbitration. Of course, guys got antsy when the talks got nasty. If you go on strike, you don't get paid. In the 50-day strike of 1981, owners really played hardball. They had 50 days worth of strike insurance while we weren't getting paid except for a couple players who had clauses in their contracts, which didn't sit well with the rest of us. So, that was the challenge for Miller and the union, and the key was for us to understand how powerful we were if we all held together. That to me was the most important thing that we needed to embrace. And really any community or any civilization that's ever been a world power, one of the first things that goes is that one-for-all mentality. Tommy Lasorda would say we all had to be pulling on the same end of the rope. Otherwise, it's chaos, and we start breaking down internally.

There were four work stoppages during my playing career—a 13-day strike at the beginning of the 1972 season, but I was still in the minor leagues; the owners' lockout of 1976, which occurred entirely during spring training; the 50-day walkout in 1981, which changed the game forever; and a two-day strike in 1985 that was not the players' finest hour. I don't remember much about 1972. I remember the 1976 spring training lockout because the owners called their shot, and the players needed to be ready to return to work, so we organized our own workouts at Vero Beach High School. Nobe Kawano, the Los Angeles Dodgers' clubhouse manager, gave us our gear so we'd have balls and bats and gloves, but we couldn't use any of the Dodgertown facilities. In 1981 action stopped midseason, and nobody worked out after that because we didn't want to embolden owners with images that the players were eager to return.

Even today's players have had to experience a work stoppage—the 2021–22 owner lockout, though most of the fight took place in the off-season. Ultimately, the start of the regular season was delayed by one week. I can't imagine how today's players can understand what happened 50 years ago. And I wouldn't want any of them to have to go through anything like our 50-day strike or the 1994 stoppage that wiped out the World Series. I just hope they realize that those battles created an economic environment that has brought them such deserved wealth. I say that because I see a generation of players who don't reflect anybody that I played with. I hope they can understand the sacrifices that we made, and that goes back well before my time to Curt Flood and even Jackie Robinson, though in recent years Robinson's story has been much better celebrated. Tell today's player stories of our $3-a-day meal money and taking broken-down buses to games, and that's got to be tough to comprehend. A player that signs a $300 million contract can't appreciate the importance of a pension. He and his family are set for life. But most of the players from my generation are living off those pensions we struck for. Those pensions have meant that a lot of ballplayers are living a dignified life in their later years that might not have been possible otherwise.

I started taking my pension two decades ago at age 53. Today, a player with 10 years of service time has a vested pension around $215,000 a year. I hope today's players and future players appreciate the hard work that resulted in this benefit for them. Players that qualify for the major league pension have in essence a golden parachute from the hard work that everybody else did. Do they appreciate it? Good question—especially with salaries soaring into the stratosphere. Who would have thought at any point in time that somebody would be paid $40 million a year to play baseball? In my day, that was not even remotely conceivable. It would have been just as likely to say you'll jump on a plane and go live on another planet.

Licensing has come a long way as well. I remember when the Topps trading card representative would come to spring training and hand us $100 checks for giving them the rights to our name, image, and likeness on their baseball card. It was such a pittance that we endorsed and stacked all of the checks in a pile, pulled out a deck of cards, and the player drawing the highest card won all the checks. At least that way somebody would have a decent payday. The first time I remember getting a check that was actually worth cashing was when I went to Chicago. That was my first year with the Cubs in 1983. The check was about $3,400. Today the union has a for-profit subsidiary, MLB Players, Inc., that manages all commercial activities of the organization. The union has more than 100 corporate partners, and the revenues are huge and growing.

Through the 1970s the pendulum, which had favored baseball owner-ship over labor for decades, began to swing our way. After several misfires by players to band together, the MLB Players Association was formed in 1966, and Miller was hired. Along with free agency, the union col-lectively bargained for a series of improvements, and with each union win, the owners grew increasingly bitter. By 1980 storm clouds were approaching, and we all had a feeling the owners were going to put their feet down and play real hardball because, as Miller told us, they were looking for a win after so many losses. Claiming that free agency and salary arbitration were killing the game (their words) by fueling salary inflation, owners sought to eliminate arbitration entirely and attach major league player compensation to any free agent leaving his team. Owners made these claims, even though attendance, revenues, and club values were soaring. The war over free-agency compensation was deferred for a season, as all other issues were resolved in a four-year collective bargaining agreement. A committee was formed to study the remaining free-agent compensation issue, and if no agreement was reached, a June 1, 1981, strike deadline was set.

The owners never believed the players would hold together in a strike. Maybe that's why it lasted as long as it did on our end. On their end, it was pretty obvious. The owners had taken out 50 days worth of strike insurance, and as soon as it ran out, we had a settlement. The owners caved, dropping demands for major league player compensation for free agency. We won a battle that benefits every player today. In his memoir, *A Whole Different Ball Game: The Sport and Business of Baseball*, Miller wrote: "Top to bottom, star to sub, liberal to conservative, the players stood firm. I was 64 years old at the time. I had been involved with labor for over 40 years, the last 15 with the Players Association. I was thinking seriously about retirement, but in the midst of this terribly stressful strike, I found it tremendously uplifting to watch the players stand their ground. Rereading the press clippings 10 years later, I'm reminded of how strong and effective and militant the Players Association had become. I'll say it again: it was the most principled strike I'd ever been associated with; it was the Association's finest hour."

I remember some guys were a little skeptical about striking, worrying about not getting paid, concerned that the owners would drop the hammer on us. But I don't recall any player adamantly opposed to what the vast majority of players knew was the morally right thing to do. I give Miller the credit. In the same way as a club can take on the personality of its field manager, I think the union membership took on the personality of its leader. We were calm and collected. He made us knowledgeable on the issues we were fighting for and had the vision for how vital it was for our future and the future of those who followed us. When you get that many people involved, you have a lot of different backgrounds, education levels, language barriers, IQs, whatever. It would be understandable if you had more than a few dissenters and outright opponents of the majority. But the union made sure that every single player understood the importance of the issues at stake, and I think most of us realized we were carving a new path, picking up the fight that Flood began in 1969 when the St. Louis Cardinals traded him to the Philadelphia Phillies.

Flood didn't want to be told where he had to work, so he filed a federal antitrust lawsuit seeking to overturn the one-sided reserve clause. Flood lost the case because of an illogical 1922 Supreme Court decision that granted baseball an antitrust exemption, establishing legal precedent still in place today. The curious decision was upheld in 1953, and the Supreme Court encouraged Congress to pass a law treating baseball like all other sports. Congress never acted. Nonetheless, Flood's brave battle awoke the union to the importance of striving for a real free agency. Miller knew the day would come that we would have to fight for a real free agency and he had us ready. He had always said to just give the owners time, make them squirm a little, and they'd go their 26 separate ways. And it went just like he said. He knew their heartbeat.

I never went through free agency, but its existence provided me with the leverage to have a say in where I would play. I never felt the restraints of the reserve clause like Flood. But I did see how players could be pushed around by the system. I saw players released just days before they would qualify for pension thresholds. And they had been counting down the days. I saw a teammate come to the clubhouse, and his locker had been emptied. "Where's my stuff?" he asked the clubhouse attendants.

He had been released, and the front office didn't have the decency to tell him. It was baseball's equivalent of changing the locks on the office door. He thought it was some kind of prank. I mean, it was cruel. Baseball can be cruel, but it doesn't have to be. They could have made a courtesy call: "Hey, come by the office before you go downstairs." They could have told him, "You've been a tremendous asset to the organization, but we had a decision to make, and unfortunately, you're on the other side of it. But we want to thank you and if we can help you in any way, we will."

I could live with that. But back then it was more like you've got 10 minutes to clear out your desk. That's almost how they made me feel when I went to arbitration. It felt like I was robbing a bank, and they were going to punish me for it. And they wonder why we held together to fight for our rights.

I knew baseball would be my career's work. But when I made that decision, it was a game. I wasn't thinking of it in business terms and I didn't realize how much of a business baseball had become until we were into one of the basic agreement negotiations, and some of the owners' books were revealed. For decades the financial numbers of baseball weren't really on the table. I guess we were a little naïve. That was a real eye-opener. Until then, we didn't know what the player in the next locker was making, and that's how the owners wanted it. It happens in all businesses, and that's the way it was in ours until the union educated us on the value of salary information. When you read the minute details of every contract a player signs, that information really isn't for the benefit of the fan. It benefits the player, so every player knows where he stands. Back in the day, the player was at the mercy of the club. Buzzie Bavasi, the late Dodgers general manager, proudly admitted to deception in his contract negotiations. He would call in a player for a one-on-one session before the days of agents. The duplicitous exec would conveniently leave a contract of a star teammate with a low salary visible on his desk and would conveniently be called away just long enough for the player to peek at the contract. Of course, the salary on the contract was bogus. It was misinformation intended to fool the player from making a legitimate salary comparison and instead accept a lowball offer. One of Miller's greatest strengths was understanding the importance of keeping his players informed in an age before cell phones, texting, and email. He used the media to get his message out to us.

When I was a rookie, it didn't seem that important to me because I figured everybody was making more than I was. Actually, I was paid $17,000 as a rookie, which was above the $13,500 minimum, and there wasn't a negotiation. The next year, Al Campanis gave me a $10,000 raise. He said he could only afford to give me the $10,000 because if it was more it would screw up the salary scale and yada, yada, yada. And for me at that point, a $10,000 increase was a big deal. I couldn't really complain about that.

Salary arbitration, which we won in the 1972 strike, opened the door for me in 1974, when Campanis and I couldn't reach an agreement. Campanis wouldn't pay me what I felt I was worth because he said I wanted the same amount that guys with six years of experience were making. Back then and to a certain extent still today, players were paid based on seniority. I threw on the table that I had 97 RBIs, was the starting third baseman in the All-Star Game, and was an integral part of the National League champions. I felt I had done more than my part, and the club needed to acknowledge that. But Campanis shifted the argument to service time ahead of production. "If I'm worth it, then why can't you pay me?" I asked.

Campanis said, "You're only a two-year player and you want to be paid like a six-year player. If I do that, it will throw the whole thing out of whack."

They were very concerned about the salary structure, but they didn't seem to understand that their argument was baseless now that the arbitration process was in place. I mean, keeping intact their salary structure really wasn't my problem.

Through arbitration we now knew the salaries of all the other players and could compare my production with everybody else. Bavasi's ploy to stack the negotiating deck was no longer possible. The process was going to land on a salary considered fair by an independent third party, negating the previous method in which club management previously had the unilateral power through the outdated reserve clause to renew a player at the salary of its choosing. The process encouraged (and still does) both sides to pick a reasonable number because to win a case you only need to convince the arbitrator that your number is one dollar closer to the midpoint of the two numbers submitted. In theory, the risk of losing by picking an outlandish number should bring both sides closer together. For example, we submitted $56,000, and the club submitted $47,000. We softened our previous ask of $60,000 to make our case easier to prove, while the club lowered its number and made its case harder to prove. I guess they thought they would penalize me for not taking the $50,000 offer, but they made our task easier. Our burden was to convince the arbitrator that the fair number was one dollar on our side of the midpoint or $51,501. The night before the hearing, Campanis called and said, "How about we go back to our original offer of $50,000?" He wanted to get it done.

I said, "Well, it's not going to work. This is why we're going to arbitration, so I won't miss any time. We'll have it decided one way or another. Either it'll be mine or it'll be yours."

I was fine letting the process play out, but that wasn't what he wanted to hear. "Okay," he said, adding a parting shot I'll never forget, "but you're going to lose."

Arbitration is now an accepted, normal part of the salary process, but it was still in its infancy back then. Nobody could predict how it would go, but I viewed it as a process not a confrontation. All I wanted was resolution on this. Some players, though, feared it. I was actually getting calls from some of the guys telling me not to do it, like, "You sure you want to rock the boat?" They were afraid there would be retaliation against me if I won. I didn't see it as a fight. This was just a fair way to resolve a difference of opinion.

As far as the mechanics of the hearing, I was in for a surprise. It was held at a hotel near Los Angeles International Airport. I was there with my attorney, Steve Schneider, and the Dodgers had Campanis, vice president Red Patterson, probably a couple of lawyers, and the arbitrator. They proceeded to tell me how lucky I was to have a locker at Dodger Stadium. They ripped into me pretty good, especially considering I was coming off an All-Star season. We didn't have the computers and sophisticated analytics they have today, so the preparation was rather primitive by today's standards. I had set a Dodgers rookie record for RBIs and didn't even know it until well after that season. Our hearing was mostly comparative statistics to other players, and I think that's what swayed the arbitrator to decide I really deserved to be paid. I got the call the next day that we won. A few weeks later at a luncheon, Walter O'Malley said to me, "Congratulations but don't ever let this happen again."

He meant it both ways, and I took it that way, meaning that we should respect the process and be fair with each other going forward. But you know what? That was also a bonding thing. From that point on, I had a closer relationship with O'Malley. With Campanis, though, not so much.

Still, the process worked. I didn't have to consider holding out, which was the only real option before arbitration. I was able to leave for spring training on time and I told my agent to make it plain and clear to the organization that we were simply using the process to determine a salary—nothing more than that. I wasn't trying to be a hard ass here. We were simply using our rights. Today, nobody worries about that. Everybody just automatically files for arbitration if it reaches a certain point. If further negotiating doesn't result in an agreement, you go to a hearing, and in one day, it's decided. In fact, now some of the clubs are the ones that take a hard stance, insisting on a hearing if a settlement isn't reached before figures are exchanged. Either way it's just a procedure. But arbitration really does allow players who have great production in their first two seasons—when they have no salary leverage—to catch up.

It's pretty funny when you think about the Dodgers taking me to arbitration over a difference of $9,000 compared to today, when the gaps between submitted numbers are in the millions. It's also funny to see a club like the Seattle Mariners give Julio Rodriguez a 14-year deal that could pay him $470 million, and he's a 21-year-old rookie. As much as the Ramirez contract makes my head spin, I'm sure Walter O'Malley is rolling in his grave at the thought of any owner guaranteeing so much to anyone—let alone a relatively unproven 21 year old who doesn't even have negotiating leverage yet. I don't understand it. There are so many random reasons why it can all fall apart for any player with such a brief track record. But it just goes to show what Miller told us all along—the money is there, or the owners wouldn't pay it. And if the owners don't pay it to the players, they'll pocket it. The players are the product and they deserve a reasonable share.

After winning the arbitration, I had a 1975 season that I had always considered was my best. I was the Dodgers' MVP, became an All-Star again, had my highest WAR ranking of 6.7, slugged 25 homers, drove in 101 runs, and hit .283. I had no idea what OPS was back then, but through today's perspective, my .845 was solid. Technically, it was the best season of my career, even though I didn't have one career-high stat. But we did not win, finishing second, 20 games behind the Big Red Machine. And to be candid, it was a season of chaos for the Dodgers. There was friction in the clubhouse for a bit, and it spilled into the public and made for sensational headlines, just the type of controversy the Dodgers of that day were insistent on avoiding at all costs. For reasons I still don't understand, it seemed like I was the poster boy for all of the bad stuff that had gone on.

I bring this up as the backdrop to my salary negotiations for the following season. Instead of holding any of that stuff against me, the Dodgers offered me the longest contract they'd ever given: three years for $350,000 through the 1978 season. The timing wasn't coincidental either. In December of 1975, arbitrator Peter Seitz ruled that Dodgers pitcher Andy Messersmith and Baltimore Orioles pitcher Dave McNally had earned free agency because their clubs invoked the reserve clause a second time by unilaterally renewing their contracts. Two minutes after issuing his ruling, Seitz was fired by the owners. But free agency had become a thing in baseball. Messersmith then rejected the Dodgers' three-year, $540,000 offer to sign with Ted Turner's Atlanta Braves for three years and $1 million. The bidding wars had begun.

To head off further auctions, the Dodgers got aggressive. In April of 1977, I had a record month, hitting .425 with nine homers and 29 RBIs. By the end of May, we were up maybe 10 games in the standings and were steamrolling. In early May, Peter O'Malley came to me and said he wanted to talk about extending my contract. I wasn't even halfway through the current three-year deal. He said he wanted to extend the current contract with five more years, taking me through 1983. In addition to the guaranteed money, it would take me into 10-year big league status, automatically giving me veto rights to any trade. How do you turn that down?

As it turned out, I did agree to a trade to the Cubs before the 1983 season, but that turned out to be another windfall for me. With one year remaining on my contract, Chicago Cubs general manager Dallas Green tore up the deal and gave me a new five-year contract commensurate with the top free agents of that year. It even included an attendance clause, which until then had been the exclusive domain of players like Reggie Jackson.

While I was with the Cubs and after Miller retired, our union veered a little off course. We struggled to find a suitable replacement for Miller. At one point we even recruited him out of retirement to take back his prior role on an interim basis. In 1985 under executive director Donald Fehr, we had another mid-season work stoppage. Maybe we were still fatigued from the 1981 debacle, but this one lasted only two days, and we agreed to give back a portion of our salary arbitration and accepted a change in pension funding. "Give backs" are dirty words to unions, and I don't think guys were real happy about going backward. You can't allow that to happen. We went back in time a little bit. Why would you want to give up anything that you've already fought for and won? It was definitely a defeat. We had fought to get arbitration for players with two years of service and we came out of this negotiation with arbitration after three years of service. Nearly 40 years later, we never fully reclaimed the two-year threshold. So, 1985 wasn't our finest hour. But it was a lesson learned about give backs.

For those 1985 negotiations, Miller was officially a consultant, though in his book he complained that union leaders had excluded him from critical sessions. Maybe Fehr just wanted to put his mark on things because it was now on his watch. Maybe Miller had a better read on the owners than Fehr. Maybe it was just the changing times. The bottom line was we took a step back. Here are Miller's recollections: "Going into the negotiations, I wasn't involved enough to notice that there wasn't the support among the players that there should have been. It was a miscalculation on my part, something I hadn't considered. I hadn't been at the spring training meetings since 1982, I hadn't attended most board meetings, I wasn't talking to player reps and other players on a daily basis. There were cracks, and they became apparent as the negotiations went on."

Miller wrote that the dramatic increase in salaries minimized the importance to players of pensions, which had always been an issue that bonded all players. There also was a "diminished concern" for younger players by older players. That left Fehr with a more difficult hand to play. "People used to tell me, 'No matter what the issue, you always had the support of the players,'" Miller wrote. "While that's true, it didn't happen of itself. I worked at it. I made sure that the players understood what I was doing, that they had input into decisions, that their reactions and ideas were seriously considered, that the information they needed to make intelligent decisions was theirs for the asking [and even when they didn't ask]. Most important of all, I made sure that they understood the struggle involved in getting what they had. I used to stress that there was more to be had, but it, too, would require a struggle. The minute we relaxed, we were greasing the skids for failure. I tried to pound this message home to the players each spring. If one side becomes complacent, the other side becomes bolder. Either you push forward or you're going to get pushed back. In the type of labor management situation in baseball, attempting to hold your ground, marking time, is an invitation to being shoved backward."

Change can be tough to deal with for anybody. In the union's case, Miller wasn't going to be executive director forever. History shows he was a hard man to replace, but it was bound to happen for better or for worse. The union must always be prepared for change. There's no way to compare the issues today's players have with what we faced. But I've learned, as the years pass, that you can't fight change. So you might as well be ready for it, even embrace it as a positive opportunity. I've told my kids if they see something around the house that needs attention, say something. We all get a little complacent in different ways. Sure enough, a few years ago, my grown daughter came to visit and said, "Dad, that bathroom needs some work. It looks like it just came out of the 1980s." She was right, and I thanked her because I hadn't seen it. Sometimes we become so comfortable with the way things are that we don't notice the flaws.

The biggest change on the horizon for baseball is legalized sports gambling. It's still unclear how baseball will share in the inevitable financial windfall, but nationwide legalization of sports gambling is destined to be the next great revenue stream for owners and players. Gambling will be the next cash cow, replacing the regional sports networks, which appeared to have peaked with the Dodgers' $8 billion deal. Whether you ethically approve of gambling or not, it's been embedded in human society. I remember my days playing winter ball at Hiram Bithorn Stadium in San Juan, Puerto Rico. Sections of the grandstand were separated by chain-link fences, but they couldn't stop gamblers from stuffing their bets through the gaps. It doesn't take a wild imagination to envision pitch-by-pitch wagers by remote control from the comfort of home or from anywhere by cellphone, not to mention from a ballpark seat. Teams are already partnering with brick-and-mortar and online casinos, so you know it's right around the corner. At the turn of the century, baseball was a $2 billion business. Now it's a $12 billion runaway Brink's truck. I don't know where it's headed, but I've seen how far it's come in my time.

• CHAPTER 14 •

SCULLY AND JARRIN

The year before my rookie season, the Los Angeles Dodgers drew 1.8 million in attendance, which was pretty good at the time. With our influx of new players and our early success, we were able to capture the fans, and they latched onto us pretty well. So we were, in essence, growing this relationship into a family. We won 95 games our first year, losing in a close divisional race to the Cincinnati Reds. The following year, we won 102 games and went to the World Series. We had four starters in the All-Star Game. Our attendance was growing as we established the young core of players, in particular the infield, that would be the foundation of our success. Fans were getting to know us and getting used to us. And I think by the time that we hit 1978, we had really established ourselves as L.A.'s team. It was our third World Series in five years, and that's a pretty abrupt turnaround. By 1982 we set a new attendance record of 3.6 million. The infielders had become household names to our fanbase, and they treated us like family. They did not boo us. When we went south a little bit, they understood, and we were able to make that correction rather quickly. It was a great relationship. Contrast that with, say, Philadelphia. It's kind of hard to imagine booing Steve Carlton, booing Mike Schmidt. That really didn't happen to us.

The players back then embraced the relationship with the fans. We had Autograph Day or Photo Day before every Sunday home game.

It might be hard to believe, considering the level of security nowadays, but all the players went to a pre-determined location in the ballpark and posed for pictures with the fans for a half hour. The only player exempt from participating was that game's starting pitcher. The fans really got a kick out of doing that, and the players realized it was our duty for the greater good of the business. Tickets were affordable compared to other forms of entertainment in the Southland. A family of four could have a day at the ballpark for $30. They didn't have to pay an arm and a leg for tickets. This was Walter O'Malley's business model: make it affordable enough to draw fans to the park. Once inside, knowing the tickets were reasonably priced, fans were willing to spend more money on food and drinks and Dodgers gear. Current economics of the game are dramatically different these days. The price for tickets at all live sports is so high that some people can't or won't spend the kind of money now charged for hot dogs and beer. I hear it from them; they feel like they're being taken advantage of. That wasn't the case back in the 1970s. We were fan friendly.

Any conversation about Dodgers fans must revolve around Vin Scully and Jaime Jarrin, our two Hall of Fame broadcasters who connected with the audience and were vital in promoting our team and sport in Los Angeles.

For English-speaking fans, Scully is the icon. The stories go back to the days in the Coliseum, when everybody brought a transistor radio to the ballpark just to hear Scully recite what was happening in front of their eyes. Down on the field, players could hear comments Scully made because every radio had the volume up high, and the sound carried like a megaphone. Players couldn't help but hear it. A lot of times, he'd be doing the play by play, and between pitches, you'd find yourself listening to his story, and it was a little distracting. You'd catch yourself and get the focus back, but it was definitely part of the game in Los Angeles. I don't remember playing anywhere else and hearing everybody listening to the radio like they did with Scully. And rightfully so—because Scully was riding a wave of popularity that only increased with each passing season. He was not only broadcasting the Dodgers, but in the 1970s and 1980s, he was also doing the national telecast and other sports like PGA and the NFL. Scully was as eloquent as it gets when broadcasting a game. He could paint a picture for you and make you feel like you were sitting right there watching this thing play out. His unique connection with the fanbase helped make the Dodgers the top dog in town, and that's saying something in Los Angeles.

I think L.A. is the top city in our country for competition of the entertainment dollar because there are so many other things that you can do here. And to be the singular thing that people wanted to do more than anything else, when you've got other sports teams, the beach, the Hollywood Bowl, the Greek Theatre, or whatever, that's an achievement. We have every form of entertainment. We've got rock stars, movie stars, TV stars, professional athletes. It's a city of stars. So, it was an amazing time for us. When I arrived, Scully had Jerry Doggett as his other broadcaster, and Scully called most of the innings. Ross Porter became the third voice, and after Doggett retired, Don Drysdale joined the booth and then Rick Monday. But the thing about Scully that was so unique was that he did his broadcast solo, and I don't know how you do that. *You're the play-by-play guy, but you're also telling stories between pitches?* Those are two distinct skillsets, but he could weave those stories around the game action off the top of his head as if it was scripted. His timing was flawless. The man had no competition. He was one of a kind. And he did this since the Brooklyn days for a total of 67 years. He literally taught the game to generations of Dodgers fans. In my early years, our games were carried on KFI, a 50,000-watt station that could be heard all over the West Coast. My parents up in Washington state would tune in to Scully and Doggett even if they had to use the car radio to get better reception. Scully was probably the most famous broadcaster in the history of sports. From his rookie days as the third man in a booth with Red Barber and Connie Desmond to his Hall of Fame induction in 1982 to his emotional retirement after the 2016 season, his story is well known.

Sadly, we lost Scully on August 2, 2022, at the age of 94. A little more than two years earlier, Scully suffered multiple injuries in a fall at home. Physically, he was never the same. In 2021 his wife of 47 years, Sandra, died after a gallant fight with ALS (Lou Gehrig's disease). In 1972 Scully's first wife, Joan, died of an accidental medical overdose. In 1994 Scully's 33-year-old son, Michael, was killed in a helicopter crash. The man had more than his share of tragedy and grief, but he never let it show when he was at the ballpark. His family held a private, invitation-only memorial a few days after Scully's death. In keeping with his personality, the service was dignified and focused on his family life, not baseball. He had 37 grandchildren, and a few of them spoke, and each was eloquent. The music was like an opera. The choir did a version of "The Prayer," the song by Celine Dion and Andrea Bocelli. It really was incredible. I think Scully would have been really happy with the way it was all done. There were plenty of baseball dignitaries present—most notably close friends Sandy Koufax, who flew in from the East Coast; former owner Peter O'Malley; and longtime coach Joe Amalfitano. Joe Torre was there. Current players, including Clayton Kershaw and Justin Turner, attended. Former players included me, Steve Garvey, and Kirk Gibson. Our broadcasters were there and probably quite a few I missed as well.

If there was a Dodgers' Mount Rushmore, I think Scully would be the No. 1 face of all time, and right next to him would be Jackie Robinson, then Walter O'Malley. And then whoever you have coming after that would be of your choice. He's an irreplaceable icon in our industry; it's just as simple as that. I don't care who you're going to bring in next or how good he's going to be; there isn't any way that the next person is going to have that impact. His blood runs through the building. I've listened to his broadcasts since I've been retired and I felt like I was sitting right next to him. I get a little emotional because he was really one of a kind. Scully changed the course of baseball. He will be forever missed.

Jarrin's story is just as impressive. He came to the United States from Ecuador in 1955, the year the Dodgers won their first World Series in Brooklyn, to pursue a broadcasting career. One of those World Series games between the Dodgers and New York Yankees was the first baseball game he saw on television. He was hired by Los Angeles' Spanish-speaking radio station, KWKW, as the news and sports director and learned baseball watching Triple A Pacific Coast League games. KWKW purchased the Spanish-language rights to broadcast Dodgers games in Los Angeles, and Jarrin joined the booth, recreating the road game play-by-play off the English broadcasts for six years. In 1965 the Spanish-language broadcasts went on the road with Jarrin being the primary voice. Twenty years ago he was joined by the lefty for whom he once interpreted, Fernando Valenzuela, and for six years by his son, Jorge. His list of accomplishments and awards is right there with Scully's, and it's topped by his 1998 Hall of Fame induction as winner of the Ford Frick Award, just like Scully. Jaime retired after the 2022 season at age 86.

Through Scully and Jarrin, the Dodgers always tried to put the players in the best light while stopping short of being "homers" or announcers who overhype the home team. They praised us, occasionally put us on a pedestal, even though at times we didn't deserve it. We had it pretty good. I was always curious about how broadcasters walk that fine line between being fair and unbiased yet work for the club. If the broadcaster is critical of a player, that word gets around. Family members are listening to the game. The player hears about it, and the word spreads. But you can't be a homer either. You've got to call the game honestly or you lose credibility with the fans. I think Scully was fair most of the time, possibly overly critical occasionally. But it goes with the territory. You can't possibly please everybody. If a hitter fails seven times out of 10, he's still in the top one percentile. The player has to have thicker skin than anyone even if the criticism comes from your own announcer. And you're your own worst critic anyway. There are games when you go into the clubhouse, and you have to stand in front of a bunch of reporters and basically tell like it is. *Yeah, I had a bad game I was 0-for-5 and punched out four times.* Most of the time when you get interviewed, it's a positive interview. So in these other cases, you have to be able to stand up and take it. It's really easy to talk when things are great, right? When you have to stand up and say, "Hey, that really didn't work out too well. I've got to be able to accept that, too," that's part of a maturing process. That's part of the growing-up process.

With Scully and our fans, we had such a great situation with the Dodgers. We had hordes of fans who were coming to watch us play, we were entertaining them, we had a great facility in Dodger Stadium. The very first time I came through the main gate, I was driving up to the hill and I saw all these palm trees and all the beauty that was in there. We had our own plane, which was envied by every player in the league. And the weather was perfect. You didn't have to play games in 30 degrees and snow. You didn't have thunderstorms. You didn't have the wind blowing from side to side. You didn't have rainouts or a lot of doubleheaders.

You didn't have game delays. You didn't get melted by the summer heat and humidity. You had fans who were going to continue to come out and support you. You're in a major market getting all the attention you could ever hope for. When you have all that, you've got to have pretty thin skin to complain about a comment by the announcer or a review on a sports page in the newspaper.

Scully was one of the dwindling links to Brooklyn. So was Vero Beach, Florida, until the Dodgers left there in 2008. Our Florida spring training facility back then was well beyond state of the art. I mean, we had everything there. We had our lodging. If you needed a ride, you could just check out a car from the front desk. We had tennis courts, a swimming pool, basketball hoops. The dining room was right next to the clubhouse. You didn't have to go into town to watch a movie because they showed movies in the auditorium each night. That sounds prehistoric in this age of Netflix and streaming, but it was a big deal to us. We had a rec center with Ping-Pong. We hung out together and bonded. And you weren't isolated from the fans. You walked around the camp, and at most what separated you from the fans was a rope, and they could get autographs and photos and say hello. That might not sound appealing to today's players, but I thought it was cool. I thought the whole experience was just incredible. Even Holman Stadium at Dodgertown was old-time baseball. The dugouts didn't even have roofs. It was open, and the people had access. They could come right behind you and start talking to you and they could see your actions and how you go about your business. The outfield was crazy. When I started, there was no outfield fence—just a berm. And when it was standing-room only, fans would be on the berm, talking to the outfielders or getting souvenirs with balls in play. They had giant palm trees out there, and Dick Allen ran into one chasing a fly ball and knocked himself out cold. There was nothing like Vero Beach.

Jarrin wasn't with the club in Brooklyn, but he probably deserves as much credit for educating and entertaining the Dodgers fanbase in Los Angeles as Scully. Jarrin has been the connection for the Hispanic audience to the Dodgers in the same fashion as Scully was to the English speakers. Jarrin's job might have been tougher because the Hispanic population in Southern California wasn't nearly as large as it is now. I think you have to credit Jarrin for making the Dodgers appealing to the growing Hispanic community, which now represents roughly half of Dodger Nation. We have Dodgers fans all over the world, especially in Spanish-language countries, and nobody is more responsible for that than Jarrin. Streaming technology allows his voice to reach an even greater audience than ever. When he retired after the 2022 season, he was the longest-tenued Spanish language broadcaster in baseball history. My whole life has been centered around longevity—marriage, living in the same house, my baseball career. But I don't know if I could have the same job for almost 70 years. It's amazing that he has the perseverance to endure.

I did not see the need to become fluent in Spanish. I wish I had had the insight to know better. I had a choice in high school for foreign language of Latin, German, or Spanish. My friends were leaning German so that's the way I went. Spanish would have been much more practical. I've been here 50 years and I'm a little embarrassed by the fact that I really didn't learn Spanish. For my baseball career and for easier communication with Hispanic players, it would have been the right move. We American players kind of expect the foreigner to learn our native language. I know it's unfair. We ask them to adapt to everything we do. It's a little arrogant, don't you think?

• CHAPTER 15 •

HOLLYWOOD

Growing up in a small-town in Washington state, I never ran into Frank Sinatra or Don Rickles. I wasn't rubbing elbows with famous people. That changed when I joined the Los Angeles Dodgers. If the TBS Superstation made the Atlanta Braves America's Team, the Dodgers were Hollywood's Team. When I was playing, the stars came out to Dodger Stadium, and they still do. Like most of us, those celebs loved baseball—back before they became famous. And what Hollywood publicist wouldn't want his or her clients crossing over into the sports world, considering the media attention that follows? We didn't have social media or TMZ back then, but Dodgers management was savvy enough to court entertainers and roll out the red carpet with complimentary choice seats and clubhouse photo ops.

Even before the Dodgers came to L.A., Walter O'Malley understood the value of star power. When the club was in a political dogfight to convince voters to pass Proposition B in 1958 that would pave the way for the construction of Dodger Stadium, the club produced a five-hour Dodgerthon on KTTV Channel 11 from the studios and then from the airport as the Dodgers team plane arrived, explaining the advantages of supporting the contract and the Dodgers in Los Angeles. As documented on Walteromalley.com, "Numerous noted celebrities, including Dean Martin, George Burns, Jerry Lewis, Ronald Reagan, Debbie Reynolds,

Joe E. Brown, and Jackie Robinson partook in the festivities favoring the Dodgers. Every major business leader and association supported Prop B. Two days later the referendum received 351,683 yes votes and passed by 25,785 votes. It was the largest non-presidential election turnout in Los Angeles history with more than 62 percent of the city's 1,105,427 voters casting ballots."

Dodgers official club historian Mark Langill, writing for the Society of American Baseball Research's website, noted that the mastermind of this cross-pollination between celebrities and sports was the legendary Danny Goodman, who ran concessions and promotions for the Hollywood Stars of the Pacific Coast League through the mid-1900s—well before the Dodgers left Brooklyn. Goodman suggested having movie stars play an exhibition baseball game because many of them—Bing Crosby, Gary Cooper, future Angels owner Gene Autry, and others—were conveniently part owners of the club. The game was an instant success.

When the Dodgers arrived in Los Angeles, they hired Goodman to work his promotional magic. Not wanting to fix something that wasn't broken, Goodman suggested the new club continue the tradition of the celebrity baseball game. O'Malley asked Goodman if he would be able to secure stars for the event. According to Langill, Goodman replied: "Are you kidding? I'll get you stars you've never heard of."

Goodman was nothing if not comfortably confident. As a member of the uber-private and celebrity-rich Friars Club in Beverly Hills, he certainly had A-list connections. The Friars Club was founded by comedian Milton Berle as a private hangout for entertaining elite. Original members included Crosby, Eddie Cantor, Jimmy Durante, George Jessel, Reagan, and Robert Taylor. Every year Goodman would tap the club's roster for the Hollywood Stars Game at Dodger Stadium, and Sinatra, Martin, Lewis, and others suited up.

A three-inning game would take the place of our pregame batting practice, and fans watched some of their favorite stars on the Dodger Stadium diamond as a warm-up act for the major league game that night. The players got a kick out of seeing these big stars trying to play their game. And, I mean, the names were the biggest names in Hollywood—Jack Benny, Sinatra, Martin, Rickles, and one of my personal favorites, Annette Funicello. All of them and many, many more would come out for Hollywood Stars Night.

Funicello might not rank with Sinatra in the eyes of most, but she did with me. When I was a kid, I came home from school and watched the Mickey Mouse Club on television, and she was everybody's sweetheart. She went on to do all of those *Beach Blanket Bingo* movies with Frankie Avalon. Everybody loved her, and I got to meet her at one of the Hollywood Stars Games. It really blew me away that all of those stars were on our field like Steve Martin, Elliott Gould, and Billy Crystal. The great Jackie Gleason was riding around in a golf cart. Okay, I admit that I get kind of starstruck. I was appearing in a celebrity golf tournament one time, and a guy was standing about 100 feet from me, and it was Avalon. To this day I kind of kick myself for not going over and saying something. But I froze. I tell this story with a little bit of passion. I wanted so much to meet Avalon. I mean, he was at the top. He sang the title song in *Grease*. I still can't believe I didn't meet him. I really haven't forgiven myself.

We had a friend, Tommy Gallagher, who was the maitre d' at Chasen's restaurant, which was one of those West Hollywood hot spots where the famous hung out. He would come to the games, visit Tommy Lasorda in the clubhouse, and invite us to come to the restaurant. It was kind of a hip place in the day. We went there one night in the offseason, and Martin and his entourage were sitting at the next table over. My wife, Fran, went nuts. I'm more on the shy side, but Fran wanted me to get his autograph. I was trying to build up enough courage to approach him, but before I knew it, Martin just got up and came over to our table. He introduced himself, and I was a little embarrassed and introduced myself, and we were talking, and he said, "I enjoy watching you play," and it's complimentary back and forth. And he ended up asking for *my* autograph. It just blew me away. I mean, *Did that really just happen? Are you kidding me? Actually, it should be the other way around, right?* He beat me to the punch there. It was just another one of those nights where it hits you how cool this whole career is. I was getting to rub elbows with these stars, and everybody knew who they were, and they even knew who we were.

Even well after I retired, that was sometimes the case. While working for the club on the business side, I was sitting in the suite of Bob Daly, the former Warner Bros. studio head who was running the Dodgers during the News Corp. years. One of his guests for that night's game was Dustin Hoffman, who is another of my all-time favorites. I was gathering up the courage to go over and introduce myself and then I realized he was coming over to me. Naturally, I said "Hi, I'm Ron Cey."

And he said, "I know who you are. You don't need to do that."

Tom Hanks was another who would frequently be in the suite, and who's a bigger star than Tom Hanks? But he's as friendly and as nice a guy as you'd ever meet anywhere. And one of the funny things I learned about Hanks is that he keeps score when he goes to games, just like a lot of hardcore fans. He would write little comments on the side of his scorecard about certain plays. His score sheet was immaculate. The point is that despite all of his stardom he acts like a regular guy. He doesn't act entitled or demand special attention.

Lasorda took the Hollywood-ization of the Dodgers to the next level. I can't remember how many times I walked past Lasorda's clubhouse office and did a double take after realizing which headliner was his pre-game or postgame guest on that night. Pictures on the walls of his office were like the Hollywood Walk of Fame. One entire wall was dedicated to pictures of Sinatra, who delivered on his promise to sing the national anthem on Opening Day of 1977 for Lasorda's first game as Dodgers manager.

Because of Lasorda, Sinatra was around quite a bit and he used to come into the clubhouse with Rickles, the headlining comedian known for insulting anybody and everybody to their face. Most of the time their visits were unannounced. They'd just show up before the game, and we'd be in the clubhouse, and here they came. Right away you knew you were about to be roasted. Rickles would start with whoever's locker was closest to the door he entered. He would just go locker to locker, ripping every guy on the team. He was viciously funny. Sinatra would stand a little to the side and laugh his ass off. Rickles was enough of a fan to know whatever you did recently that wasn't up to par and he would zing you. If you didn't get a bunt down, he'd ask, "Who taught you how to bunt?" If you had airmailed a throw over home plate, he would say, "That throw from left field last night get away from you a little bit?" And, of course, I was easy pickings. "Hey, Penguin, nice range on that ground ball. Glad you made an attempt at it since it was, what, two feet away?" And then he would imitate me with a couple Penguin waddle steps and fall over imitating my dive. It was all meant in his style of humor. He made sure he had something to say about everybody, and everybody was pretty much in stitches. It became pretty routine. You'd see him walk in and wonder, *What he's going to have to say about last night or what is he going to say about me?*

He could get under your skin if you had the wrong temperament, and I saw that once during the Frank McCourt era. We were at a banquet, and Frank and Jamie McCourt were getting a humanitarian award at the Beverly Hilton. Al and Tipper Gore were there, and Rickles said something about Tipper Gore that did not go over well. And when Al Gore came up to speak, he addressed the comments Rickles made, and it was pretty awkward. Gore didn't slap Rickles like Will Smith did to Chris Rock, but you could feel the tension. Rickles' humor was a much better fit in the clubhouse, where he had carte blanche that comedians need. In the clubhouse nothing's sacred or politically incorrect. And you're supposed to just kind of laugh it off, I guess. That said, never underestimate ballplayer humor. Rickles did, and one time we got our pound of flesh. Four of us lifted Rickles and dumped him into a dirty clothes hamper. That time, we got the last laugh.

When Rickles was done roasting the roster, he and Sinatra and their entourage went into Lasorda's office, and it was like an Italian restaurant in there. That spread got larger and larger as the years went by. Lasorda's office was pretty much the clubhouse dining room before and after games. When the players were full, Lasorda would offer the leftovers to the media during his postgame conference. Believe me: everybody appreciated the quality food Lasorda's restauranteur friends would bring because Nobe Kawano, our clubhouse manager, supplied crackers and peanut butter and not much more. It wasn't like it is now with a full-scale restaurant in the clubhouse and a dedicated chef, dietician, and smoothie bar.

The first big-name celebrity I remember seeing with the Dodgers wasn't Sinatra; it was Danny Kaye. In addition to his acting, singing, and dancing, Kaye was a lifelong Dodgers fan who was an original investor in the Seattle Mariners. He was a close friend of the O'Malleys, who would regularly host him at spring training. We have a picture with my mom, my mother-in-law, and my father-in-law with Kaye at the Vero Beach Christmas party.

The most famous people I had ever met before reaching the major leagues were retired ballplayers. I couldn't have been 10 years old when I went to an NBA exhibition game at the University of Puget Sound. I was playing in a basketball league, and we played as the pregame show. Our bonus was seats behind the bench for the NBA game. We were sitting behind Bill Russell (of the Boston Celtics, not my future teammate) and Bill Sharman, and Sharman's autograph ended up being my first autograph ever. I got it on a torn piece of my brown lunch bag. And I remember taking it home, and you know it's just a jagged piece of paper. And I remember sticking it in my clothes drawer for safe keeping. It was such crazy fun to watch these guys play.

When I accepted the award for the 1971 Minor League Player of the Year in the state of Washington, I got to meet Billy Martin and Ron Santo. Because Santo was one of the best third basemen ever, meeting him was very special and became more special as time went on. I certainly knew in the moment what was going on, but we developed a real relationship as the years passed. I was sometimes compared to Santo and then I played with the Chicago Cubs and got to know him on another level as he was part of the Cubs organization. I treasure a picture taken of us in Wrigley Field behind the batting cage. He's on the third-base side, I'm on the first base side, and we're both looking back toward our dugouts with No. 10 jerseys. After I retired as a player, he was still doing Cubs radio. So when the Cubs would come to Dodger Stadium, I'd go up to the booth and always say hello. I was very proud of my friendships, being able to know players like Santo or Willie Mays, my personal favorite player of all time. I got to see Mays play in an exhibition game when I was maybe 12 years old when the Giants came up to

Washington to play their Triple A affiliate, the Tacoma Giants. That's when I got to see the "Say Hey Kid" in real life. I still get chills thinking about that day. Then to be able to play against him and become friends with him—it doesn't happen very often in life when you get to interact on that level with your heroes.

If Mays was my childhood baseball idol, Fleetwood Mac was my rock-and-roll equivalent. I got to know the band in the strangest way. Judy Wong was the band's traveling secretary. She noticed that my nickname was Penguin. Coincidentally, the band's logo is a penguin. She contacted the Dodgers' public relations department to see if we could do something together, and it was the start of a relationship that continues today.

Wong is a sweetheart, always in a good mood, and the one who pretty much was concierge to the band. One day she called to ask if the band could come to the clubhouse and meet the players. When they came they brought me a director's chair with "Penguin" on it. Back then we didn't even have chairs in the clubhouse. We had wooden lockers with a storage bin in it and on top of the bin was a wooden bench with hinges. If you needed to sit, you sat on that wood bench inside your cubicle. Now every clubhouse has director's chairs or lounge chairs in front of every locker. After the band's gift, I was the only one with a chair, but that didn't last long. After I got mine, a lot of the players started badgering our clubhouse guy, Kawano, to get director's chairs in there for everybody. So that one chair started a trend to have director's chairs in clubhouses. It fit our Hollywood style anyway.

When Fleetwood Mac was putting together its album *Tusk* in the late 1970s, the band invited me to sit in on a few of their recording sessions in Santa Monica. Mick Fleetwood and Lindsey Buckingham used to do most of the mixing, and it was quite a learning process because I got to see how they did it. I was always curious how you did that stuff. And

I listened to John McVie, the guitarist, doing his part over what had already been Stevie Nicks' singing and Christine McVie's singing, and it was really an amazing experience. The USC marching band played on the album's title song, and they filmed part of the video at Dodger Stadium.

A couple of years ago, our family went to Maui, and I got ahold of Mick Fleetwood, who lives there and owns a very popular restaurant in Lahaina called Fleetwood's, and he couldn't have been nicer. He came to our table, took pictures, set up my kids to go to a New Year's Eve party while Fran and I babysat the grandkids. He's been great over the years, and I've always been grateful. One of my favorite Fleetwood Mac stories occurred when I was still playing in L.A. Wong called us one night in the offseason and asked if we were doing anything. She said Eric Clapton was playing unannounced at a club in Hollywood with Fleetwood Mac in a few hours and asked if we would like to go.

I said, "We're on our way." Clapton was supposed to go on stage around 11:00 PM. But first there was going to be a so-called opening act—Robin Williams. We were about to go in, and here came Williams jaywalking across Sunset Boulevard—not in a crosswalk but in the middle of the street, and cars were stopping, and drivers were yelling his name and honking, and it was just bedlam in a good way. Inside, Williams came out for his performance, and it was one of the funniest, raunchiest performances I've ever seen, and everyone was on the floor. He was hysterical. And then Fleetwood Mac played, and Clapton joined them. It was priceless.

It's fascinating how athletes and show business entertainers have a unique admiration and respect for each other. You see them connecting over generations, and it's still true today. I think that athletes are appreciative of the unique skills these entertainers have and vice versa. I think I'm more enamored with a different side of entertainment than sports. When I look at rock stars playing in a band, playing an instrument, I'm just in awe. I don't know how to do that. It's just amazing. I don't think I was the only baseball player who fantasized about playing baseball during the season and touring with a rock band in the offseason. Not that I had the talent to do what the guys in the band did, but what a life that would be.

I had enough of a taste of that when the Cubs invited me back to Wrigley Field to sing "Take Me Out to the Ballgame" in 2012. I've played before huge crowds, but that was the first time I ever had a microphone in my hand and looked out at a full stadium of people, who were looking up at me in the press box. It hit me squarely in the face. I was on stage, out there like some rock star. It was overwhelming in a sense. You can't hear yourself. You can't call timeout to start over. It's live, and you get one shot at it. And you finish by saying, "Go Cubbies," and you throw your cap out to the fans below. It was a great experience, but I think I made the right career choice.

The closest I came to hitting the charts was in 1976, when I actually cut a pair of studio recordings for Long Ball Records—"One Game at a Time" and "Playing the Third Base Bag." Don't even ask where they appeared on the Billboard charts. As I once told an interviewer, "Obviously, I was not a candidate for American Idol." My television resume was only slightly more legit. The most exposure I enjoyed was on a Miller Lite beer commercial in 1988 with future Hall of Fame broadcaster and natural funnyman Bob Uecker. I still have a case of the beer they gave me in our garage. In 1981 I made a commercial for Wheaties. I also appeared in written roles for episodes of *Columbo* with Peter Falk. (I still get residuals of 30 cents a year!) I was on Richard Pryor's *Pryor's Place*, on *Murder She Wrote* with Angela Lansbury, and as Detective Hoberman in *The Winged Serpent*. And I appeared as myself in a handful of other shows, among them *ER, Hardcastle and McCormick, Simon & Simon*, a Pearl Bailey Special, *Looking for Oscar, American Restoration*, and *Lead with Love*. I treasure these experiences.

CHAPTER 16

ONE IN A MILLION

From the start, I believed I would be a successful major league player. And from the start, my wife believed in me. In Fran, I was fortunate enough to have found a woman who was educated, strong, independent, and completely supportive. It's not easy being a baseball wife. When you look at our schedule back then and compare it to today's, we were gone a lot more. The schedule wasn't kind. The teams in our National League West division included Atlanta and Cincinnati. I don't know what part of Atlanta was west. Major League Baseball must have been using a map from the days of Columbus. When we did road trips, we were gone 10 days, two weeks, or longer. And that's a lot of time to burden your spouse with all those duties that you would have been responsible for while she's carrying her own load. Fran did it without complaint. She raised the kids. She ran the house. And when I would return from a trip, she understood that the last thing I wanted to do was go out to dinner—even if that was the first thing she wanted to do. Even during homestands, I wasn't home that much. Our games started at 8:00 PM back then. And the Los Angeles traffic, of course, always sucked. I left the house for the ballpark early in the afternoon, and most of the players stayed in the clubhouse long after the game ended. We had interviews to do and we weren't rushing out after the game like players do today. We probably stayed in there for at least an hour. Nowadays, it's much more efficiently managed by the club. Interviews are conducted one player at a time in a press conference setting, and less time is required of the players. When you have success like we had, you're going to get interviewed after the game. And we felt that was a positive and we were glad that we were able to have as much attention as we did even in those times when we had no social media at all. It was mostly newspapers, radio, and a couple local TV channels. Fran and I found a way to make it work for more than half a century, thanks mostly to her.

Here's how it began.

After playing the 1970 season for Double A Albuquerque, I headed to Arizona for instructional league and lived in Mesa with a few of the Los Angeles Dodgers players. My childhood friend and fraternity brother, Terry Croghan, was living in Tempe, Arizona, and going to law school at Arizona State. His wife, Teddi, also had gone to school with us at Washington State. They lived in an apartment complex a couple of blocks off the main drag. Teddi was telling me about this great girl who lived next door and was going to grad school at ASU. One day I asked Teddi about this girl I saw walking by the pool. She said, "That's the one I was telling you about: Fran Fishbein."

"So, that's the one? Wow!" I said. "Yeah, I'd like to meet her. Quickly."

Fran and I started dating, and the relationship took off from there. When the instructional league season was over around the beginning of December, I went home to Seattle to spend time with my best friend, Rick Austin, in a community called Northgate. Fran's semester ended around the same time, and she went home to Chicago to be with her parents for the holidays before coming to Seattle to see me. I found out later that when she went home she told her parents that she met the guy she was going to marry. She told them about me and how I was single-minded about playing baseball for a living but was still in the minor leagues at that point. Her father was rather skeptical as you might imagine, and I later learned that he said to her: "Do you realize that there is about a one-in-a-million chance of him making it? Are you sure you know what you're doing?"

And Fran told him, "This is the first guy I've met that actually has an understanding of what he's going to do with his life, and I believe him. I'm convinced he's going to be successful."

Fran's father said what I know most people believed about my career path—one in a million. That didn't bother me. I knew the odds. For every player who makes a living from professional baseball, there are thousands upon thousands who fail. You always hear that you can't do it. You're not good enough, not tall enough, don't weigh enough, don't run fast enough, can't throw hard enough. None of that mattered because I knew I was going to make it. I just had tunnel vision and I was able to block out a lot of that and just say, "I don't care. Knock me down, distract me, whatever." I believed I'd make it. In Fran I had a partner who believed it just as much as I did. I was determined. It was something I wanted so badly. It worked out, though I wouldn't recommend taking my route. But I would recommend having a partner like Fran on the journey.

Fran came to Seattle in January of 1971 to spend time with me and meet my parents. They were thrilled and impressed with who she was and pleased that their son had found someone like that. A few nights later, Fran and I went to dinner at a really nice restaurant called Ray's Boathouse, which is down near the locks in the Ballard District. This was the night I planned to pop the question, but I got cold feet. I was just kind of mumbling and I was all over the place. And finally she said, "Listen, I've had enough. Wasn't this the night that you were supposed to propose to me? Aren't you going to ask me to marry you?"

And I said, "Yeah, I think so," or something like that.

And she said, "What do you mean? Are we getting married or not?"

And I said, "Yeah." So, she was the one who asked. She took the lead, and we finished it off with cherries jubilee for dessert. And the wedding planning began.

The next spring training was the first one I showed up on time without having the military commitment or college classes. It was when Tommy Lasorda told me I'd be his third baseman at Triple A even if I didn't get a hit all spring. I ended up having a great spring and I was better prepared than at any point in time at this early stage. In fact, I was overprepared. We played .500 ball as a team, but personally I was having a breakout year after having come off the major league roster. Fran finished her first year of grad school in social work and she came to Spokane, Washington, to spend a few months with me, including our one-week trip playing in Hawaii, which was a bonus. We had a ball, and the team did well. By the end of August, she went home to Chicago to prepare for the wedding, which was set for September 11. And on September 3, Lasorda told me I was going to the big leagues. It was a whirlwind; the two most important events in my life were about to happen a week apart.

On the baseball side, I had just fulfilled a dream, reaching the major leagues. But now I was facing another major challenge. I had to meet Fran's parents, which I finally did two days before the wedding. It turned out that my father-in-law was a great guy. He and Bettie, Fran's mom, had a knack for knowing what to do and say and never interfered in the way I heard other in-laws did. I had no in-law horror stories. They were great people. Even though my future father-in-law wasn't too sure about my career choice, I understood he was just trying to protect his daughter. Fran told him she loved me to pieces and that she believed in me and that I was going to make it. And if I didn't make it, she felt I would find another successful path. She was able to get her father to turn the corner on the doubt issue. I don't know if she changed his mind about the one-in-a-million thing, but we never had any disagreements. Fran and I got married at The Drake Hotel in downtown Chicago. There were about 250 people invited, including my parents, my brother, and my best man, Austin. The wedding was a blur. I said, "I do," and early the next morning, we left for Arizona, and I dropped Fran off in Scottsdale, Arizona, for her second year of grad school. The next day I was back on a plane to San Francisco to rejoin the Dodgers. The rest of that month, we saw each other on weekends. At the end of October, I decided to play another stint of winter ball.

Fran's parents visited us in Arizona, enjoying becoming more active in our lives. In fact, I'm lucky to have had the in-laws I had. They just had a comfortable way about them. My mother-in-law actually wore a T-shirt to Wrigley Field that read: "I'm Ron Cey's Mother-In-Law." I especially appreciated that they never had a problem with my religion being different than theirs. I am Protestant, and Fran's Jewish. They had already experienced a child marrying out of the faith with Jim, Fran's brother, so that wasn't a big deal to them. I was accepted completely into their family. In return I was able to introduce them to a completely different kind of life, a door they had never been through. They were at Dodger Pines, playing golf during spring training. They were meeting famous entertainers like Danny Kaye at Dodgertown parties. They played golf with Sy Berger from the Topps baseball card company. My mother-in-law even convinced Berger to make an extra card with me that became a future third-basemen card. Instead of the original rookie card with me and Bernie Williams and Ben Oglivie, this one had me and Mike Schmidt and Dave Hilton.

Despite growing up as Chicago White Sox fans from the South Side, my in-laws became completely engaged with the Dodgers. They ended up buying a condo on the beach in Vero Beach, Florida. On our first trip into Chicago in my rookie year, Ferguson Jenkins was pitching against us. He was the Chicago Cubs' ace, a future Hall of Famer. I hustled about 20 tickets behind the visiting dugout from Billy DeLury, our traveling secretary, for family and friends. They'd never seen me play in person, and I hit a home run off Jenkins my first time up. It just went from good to unbelievable. I had some really good games in Chicago. Andy Messersmith was pitching, and I saved a shutout with a diving stop. We defeated the Cubs 10–0, and I drove in seven with two home runs. When I went back to their house, they were flipping through all the local news channels at 6:00 and 10:00 to catch the sports reports. It was amazing to have that kind of support and it only got better. It was just wonderful to be able to give them something like that at a stage in life where it was completely new.

Fran's family really taught me how wonderful family could be. Growing up, mine was dysfunctional. Fran's had their issues, too, but they handled things together. They got along. They were and are pretty special. They showed it in the bad times as well as the good. I watched the way they executed the estate of Fran's mom. It was gut-wrenching watching Alzheimer's take her, but it was a blessing to see how her family made all of the final arrangements. There were no arguments, no distrust. Just family love with dignity. I just feel I was really, really, really, really fortunate to become part of that family.

Fran and I decided early on we wanted to have a family of our own, but timing was important. I wanted to establish myself as a major leaguer first, and she wanted to utilize her degree in social work and put it to use. While I played baseball, she was hired as a social worker by the Florence

Crittenton Center in Eagle Rock near Dodger Stadium. The Florence Crittenton Center's mission is to help at-risk teens, pregnant teens, and mothers with babies. Two years into our marriage, I was the Dodgers' third baseman, Fran's career had been launched, and Daniel was born. Three years later, Amanda was born. By that time I was established, and Fran had transitioned into a different role with Florence Crittenton. The Arizona-based organization is nationwide, but each individual chapter is responsible for its fund-raising, and Fran took on that role for the Los Angeles chapter. She recruited a number of women she had met outside of baseball and also other players' wives, and they launched a series of charity events.

The most popular event was a fashion show, and she encouraged everyone to participate and even got some of the wives and their husbands modeling on the runway. When we went to Chicago, she did basically the same thing for Cubs Care, the club's charity arm. She did a really terrific job of getting actively involved, and I'm so proud of her because that tells you a little bit about who she is. And trust me: the Dodgers and Cubs were extremely grateful for her participation and helping them grow as organizations as well as giving them a presence in the community. She deserves a lot of credit for that.

The kids made our lives complete. We were fortunate that we had an open clubhouse with the Dodgers, and the kids absolutely loved going to spring training. They had to do well in school to be allowed to go to Florida for six weeks. And they took to that. I mean, it was no problem once those rules were established. They received six weeks of homework from the school and got it done in less than half that time. And when they came home from spring training, they were ahead of the curve. They had the time of their lives and they loved hanging out in Vero. Can you imagine? I mean, you go over to Dodgertown, you have this facility, and you can just run free. They would do stretching exercises with us. Our trainer, Bill Buhler, had us doing Hula-Hoop exercises, and the kids would join us. They would ride around in the golf cart with Lasorda. The Christmas party, the Western BBQ, and the St. Patrick's Day party were all fun functions and came about because of the guidance of the O'Malley ownership. These kids were in heaven, and they all still talk about it.

And when I got to the Cubs, our son, being a little older, would come to spring training in Arizona. Eventually, Daniel would be drafted in the third round out of University of California, Berkeley by the Minnesota Twins and play professional baseball, reaching Triple A. It's not uncommon for boys to follow in their baseball-playing father's footsteps. When you grow up in a major league clubhouse as Daniel did, it's no surprise. When we got to Chicago, he wore his Cubs uniform every single day. He'd wake me up at 7:00 in the morning, saying it's time to go to the ballpark. And he'd ask for $5.02 to buy lunch. He and the other kids had a routine: they'd run across the street from Wrigley Field to the McDonald's and make a massive order. He knew his order for the chicken nuggets, fries, and a drink would cost $5.02, and then they would get orders from the players and pocket the tips. He also took the broken bats and sold them to the bleacher bums. He was an entrepreneur. Daniel and I used to go out to the field before the game. I used to throw batting practice to him in left field. I remember he hit balls into the bleachers, and the fans went crazy. They loved it. The kids got to shag fly balls in the outfield, especially in spring training. Daniel and the kids used to put on a show out there catching fly balls. The kids would play stickball in the clubhouse at Wrigley Field, and our clubhouse manager, Yosh Kawano, would get furious because they usually would break a half-dozen or so lightbulbs. Except for Kawano, everyone had a lot of fun.

Think about it: we're living in a Chicago high-rise building. Fran was from Chicago; we got married at the Drake hotel. Fran had a number of women, who she went to school with at the University of Wisconsin, nearby. And we had friends in our building. Her mom and dad had their place on Bellevue, and they went to the games all the time. The kids were living the dream. Daniel got to go on the road to just about everywhere. I remember taking him to New York. We had a late game, and after the game—since the Mets had maybe the worst clubhouse food in the league—I took him to the Stage Deli. It was around midnight and it was crowded. He ordered—he always had bigger eyes than his stomach—all this stuff and then he said, "Yeah, I want the strawberry cheesecake." One slice of New York cheesecake is like 10 pounds. He got halfway through and he's struggling but was trying to get it all down. Finally, he couldn't eat anymore. We got back to the hotel, and he wanted to watch TV. He thought this was an all-night hangout, but I had to get to sleep fast because there's a day game the next day. When that alarm rang the next morning, he couldn't figure out what was going on. Sometimes he forgot that baseball was a job!

Our daughter, Amanda, followed her own path. She took a serious interest in tennis, playing United States Tennis Association tournaments on the weekends. Fran would attend Daniel's games and Amanda's tennis tournaments, driving both to practices daily. Amanda received a tennis scholarship to the University of Wisconsin (Fran's alma mater) but transferred to University of California, Santa Cruz after her first semester. Blame the boyfriend, who is long gone. Now she runs her own corporate events and retreat business. Amanda and Daniel have provided us total joy with the arrivals of grandchildren Sofia and Julian (Daniel's) and Aya and Ava (Amanda's). They are the lights of our retirement years.

• CHAPTER 17 •

WHERE ARE THEY NOW?

Dusty Baker—After 19 seasons as a player, he became the first African American manager with more than 2,000 wins. He currently manages the Houston Astros.

Bobby Castillo—He died at age 59 from cancer on June 30, 2014.

Joe Ferguson—After retiring as a player, he coached in the major leagues and managed in the minor leagues.

Terry Forster—He lives in Santee, California.

Steve Garvey—He is focused on media production, sports marketing, and personal appearances.

Dave Goltz—He returned to Minnesota to work in real estate, then insurance.

Jerry Grote—After stints of minor league coaching and broadcasting, he now owns several businesses in the San Antonio, Texas, area.

Pedro Guerrero—He managed and coached in Mexico after his playing days, was acquitted of drug conspiracy charges in 2002 and in 2017, and then survived a stroke that put him in a coma.

Burt Hooton—He has been a minor league and college pitching coach.

Steve Howe—He died on April 28, 2006, at age 48 from an auto accident. An autopsy indicated he had methamphetamine in his system.

Jay Johnstone—He died on September 26, 2020, at age 74 from complications of COVID-19 while in a nursing home for dementia.

Ken Landreaux—He coaches at MLB Urban Youth Academy in Compton, California, and is a member of Dodgers Alumni.

Davey Lopes—He coached in the big leagues from 1992 to 2017, including a two-year stint as Milwaukee Brewers manager.

Candy Maldonado—After retiring as a player, he was a Spanish-language broadcaster for ESPN.

Mike Marshall—He has held managing and front-office roles in several independent leagues and recently was assistant head baseball coach at New Mexico Highlands University.

Bobby Mitchell—He has been a minor league manager and coach.

Rick Monday—He has been a baseball broadcaster, beginning with the San Diego Padres and returning to the Los Angeles Dodgers in 1993 to replace Don Drysdale after the Hall of Famer's sudden death.

Tom Niedenfuer—He and his actress wife, Judy Landers, had a production company for children's television shows.

Alejandro Pena—He was a Dodgers minor league pitching coach from 2010 to 2013.

Jack Perconte—He teaches youth baseball and has written four books on baseball, coaching, and parenting.

Ted Power—He coached in the major and minor leagues for the Cincinnati Reds.

Jerry Reuss—He has been a broadcaster in the major and minor leagues.

Ron Roenicke—After managing the Brewers and Boston Red Sox, he's back with the Dodgers as a special assistant to the general manager.

Bill Russell—After playing 21 seasons—all with the Dodgers—he managed the club from 1996 to 1998. For the last 15 seasons, he has been an MLB umpire evaluator.

Steve Sax—He currently is a broadcaster with MLB Network on Sirius/XM and motivational speaker after having coached two seasons for the Arizona Diamondbacks.

Mike Scioscia—After managing the Angels for 19 years, he managed Team USA to a silver medal in the 2020 Olympics.

Reggie Smith—He runs a baseball academy in Encino, California, and has held repeated stints as hitting coach for the U.S. Olympic Team.

Dave Stewart—He has been a general manager and player agent.

Rick Sutcliffe—He has served as an ESPN analyst since 1998.

Derrell Thomas—After coaching in independent ball and high school, he's now a member of the Dodgers Alumni.

Fernando Valenzuela—Since 2003 he has been a Spanish-language broadcaster with the Dodgers and has owned the Tigers de Quintana Roo of the Mexican League since 2017.

Gary Weiss—He is the vice president of a Texas insurance company.

Bob Welch—Previously the pitching coach for Arizona Diamondbacks, he died June 9, 2014, at age 57 from a broken neck suffered in an accidental bathroom fall.

Steve Yeager—Now part of the Dodgers Alumni, he had served for nearly a decade as a Dodgers catching instructor.

ACKNOWLEDGMENTS

Steve Schneider became my agent and attorney in 1974 and was with me through my entire Major League Baseball career. I am grateful for your countless contributions along the way. Felix Harke, my fraternity brother at Washington State University, has been a great asset in my life as a friend and confidant. Rick Austin was my childhood baseball buddy. We shared the same goals, and your drive, ambition, focus, and dedication made it easy for me to stay on track and in pursuit of my childhood dream. For nearly a half century, publicist Steve Brener has provided countless hours of dedication representing the Dodgers and has been a true friend. Mark Langill, the Dodgers' in-house historian, constantly amazes me with an encyclopedic knowledge of Dodgers history. I have always enjoyed our conversations and friendship and truly appreciate your guidance in this project. Brent Shyer, vice president at O'Malley Seidler Partners, has provided indispensable assistance in all phases of this book. Rich Kee, one of the Dodgers' team photographers while I was playing, has been an invaluable resource in curating the photographs used in the book.

While remembering my old stories and ensuring they were correct, the following resources were helpful: Baseball-reference.com, Walteromalley. com, MLB.com, Sabr.org, *Los Angeles Times, Los Angeles Herald-Examiner*, Baseball America's *The Baseball Draft*, Marvin Miller's *A Whole Different*

Ball Game: The Sport and Business of Baseball, Bowie Kuhn's *Hardball: The Education of a Baseball Commissioner*, Fred Claire's *My 30 Years in Dodger Blue*, Buzzie Bavasi's *Off the Record*, Bill James' *Best Players of the Last 50 Years*, Paul Olden's recording of Tommy Lasorda on Dave Kingman's performance, and Les Grobstein's recording of Lee Elia on Chicago Cubs fans.

Special thanks to John Nikas, who helped get this project started. I thank Steve Young for your persistent encouragement that I had a story to tell. It wouldn't have happened without you. And to Ken Gurnick, I am so pleased that we were able to reconnect to do this book and I am grateful for your expertise, insight, and contributions to make this happen.

ABOUT THE AUTHORS

Ron Cey was a six-time All-Star third baseman and an integral part of the Los Angeles Dodgers as they won four National League pennants in an eight-year span. He capped a 17-year Major League Baseball career with World Series MVP Award honors when the Dodgers captured the 1981 World Series. He was a member of the longest-running infield in MLB history. After retiring as a player, Ron worked with the Dodgers in a variety of marketing and business roles. He lives with wife Fran in Woodland Hills, California.

Ken Gurnick skipped second-grade class to attend the first game played at Dodger Stadium in 1962 and has followed the Dodgers ever since. He covered the Dodgers beat for nearly four decades, the last 20 seasons for MLB.com, before retiring after the Dodgers won the 2020 World Series. He coauthored *Tales from the Los Angeles Dodgers Dugout* with Rick Monday and *My Bat Boy Days* with Steve Garvey. He lives with wife Sheryl in Oak Park, California.